Red Dead Redemption

Red Dead Redemption

Matt Margini

Boss Fight Books
Los Angeles, CA
bossfightbooks.com

Copyright © 2020 Matt Margini
All rights reserved.

ISBN 13: 978-1-940535-24-1
First Printing: 2020

Series Editor: Gabe Durham
Associate Editor: Michael P. Williams
Book Design by Cory Schmitz
Page Design by Christopher Moyer and Lori Colbeck

For Raymond and Nicholas

CONTENTS

WESTERN

"THE *WEST* WOULD FREAK YOU OUT! You would call yo' momma!"

Someone said that to me four years ago, and I remember feeling that weird déjà vu you feel when a moment in your life becomes a movie. He was the Stranger; I was the city kid, taken by the railroad to a world I couldn't survive. In truth, he was a professor, a theory-head titan with a mane of shaggy hair, a folksy drawl, and a somewhat dastardly-looking mustache. He wasn't even from the West; he was from the South. What's more, we were sitting in a French brasserie on the Upper West Side that was crawling with wine-guzzling academics—not exactly a saloon. Nevertheless, he took one look at me and it was clear that I'd barely been past the Hudson, let alone the Mississippi. There's an old *New Yorker* cover that depicts what the rest of the world looks like to a certain kind of provincial Manhattanite: After rows of densely detailed and peopled blocks, you see a strip of orange called Jersey, and then a plain of blankness encompassing everything from Kansas to California to Asia and beyond. That was my view. I'd never seen the Grand Canyon, or the sun set over the Pacific; the only time I'd seen the desert had been as a vast expanse on *Breaking Bad*. Aside from a weekend trip to Lake Tahoe for the *Hot Tub Time Machine* college press junket (long story) and a two-night stay in the middle of downtown Phoenix, I still haven't been to the West at all—which should probably make me disqualified to write this book.

But this isn't a book about the West. It's a book about the "West" that lives in the imagination of Easterners, myself included, and it's a book about one video game in particular that has brought that space to life for millions of players: *Red Dead Redemption*. Developed by Rockstar Games, the studio best known for the Grand Theft Auto series, and released on May 18, 2010, *Red Dead* is both one of the most critically and commercially successful video games of all time and perhaps the most effective simulation of the West ever created. (It might still be, since *Red Dead Redemption 2*, Rockstar's massive 2018 prequel, takes place mostly in a vision of America's east-of-the-Mississippi heartland.) The game lets you roam on horseback across locales transposed from every kind of Western movie: ranches and valleys and long, flat desert expanses; homesteads and ghost towns and night towns and burgeoning frontier cities. It lets you do almost anything—moral or immoral—you might've seen a gunslinger do. You can lasso a wild horse, lead cattle to pasture, draw your pistol for a duel in the middle of town. You can cheat at cards, rob the bank, hijack and blow up a moving train. You can hunt all manner of animals and people—sometimes for money, sometimes for justice, sometimes just for the hell of it. You can be the force of the law in a lawless land; more often, you'll find yourself running from it.

In *Red Dead* you play as John Marston, a lanky, leathery gunfighter with a voice that sounds like it's coming out of an exhaust pipe. The year is 1911, decades after the closing of the frontier and twelve years after the heyday of Marston's old gang (whose travails are depicted in *Red Dead Redemption 2*). Captured by the U.S. government for prior offscreen sins, Marston is forced to hunt down the gang's principal players—Bill Williamson, Javier Escuella, and the charismatic ringleader of them all, Dutch van der Linde—while his wife and son remain in custody. He hunts Bill in New Austin, a rough frontier state where he encounters the kindness of some—like Bonnie MacFarlane, a rancher who saves his life—and the derangement of others. The hunt for Escuella takes him down into Nuevo Paraíso, the game's version of Mexico, where he finds himself unwittingly entangled with both sides in a revolutionary conflict. He confronts Van der Linde in a more modernized state called

West Elizabeth—chases him to the edge of a cliff high up in the mountains, at which point the silver-tongued outlaw, weary of the death of the West, decides to jump. Marston heads home to his wife, Abigail, and his son, Jack, and the game allows you to feel for a moment that he's achieved the redemption promised in the title. For a few missions, he simply helps out around the ranch, rebuilding the quiet lifestyle that, for the whole game—for his whole life—he fought for. But then the government comes knocking. At the game's inescapable climax, federal agents corner him at his ranch and pump him full of bullets, leaving his son, Jack, to assume the mantle of a dying breed.

The story of *Red Dead*'s development begins with 2004's *Red Dead Revolver*, a Western-themed third-person shooter that Rockstar acquired the rights to when it bought Angel Studios, a small San Diego-based developer, and turned it into Rockstar San Diego. As documented by Blake Hester for Polygon, the history of *Revolver* is interesting in its own right: half-developed by Angel and half-developed by Capcom, its initial Japanese publisher, the game seesawed throughout its development between a more gritty and realistic Western aesthetic (preferred by Angel) and a more absurd, vaguely Occidentalist fever dream (preferred by Capcom). "One of the characters that they had in the game, they wanted him to be this big, giant sort of Frankenstein-looking guy who was wearing a dress," recalls Daren Bader, *Revolver*'s art director. The realistic aesthetic won out when Rockstar acquired the studio in 2002. CEO Sam Houser and his brother Dan, Rockstar's VP of Creative, had been interested in making a Western for a while; now they had a chance to acquire one that was almost finished. But *Revolver* had some limitations—it was arcade-y, broken into levels, and amounted to little more than a fun and fast-paced shooter. It wasn't long after the release of *Revolver* that, in 2005, they started making the Western they really wanted to make.

Red Dead Redemption took over five years to develop and drew on the skills of more than 800 people who worked for both Rockstar San Diego (the primary development studio) and other Rockstar studios across multiple continents: Rockstar Leeds, Rockstar Lincoln, Rockstar North. Like *Red Dead Redemption 2*, which incited controversy in October 2018 after Dan Houser boasted about the "100-hour workweeks" the studio had demanded of some of its employees, the first *Redemption* was likely the product of grueling labor conditions, which are difficult to describe due to Rockstar's notorious combination of secrecy and litigiousness. As David Kushner recounts in *Jacked: The Outlaw Story of Grand Theft Auto*, in early 2010, a group of self-identified "Determined Devoted Wives of Rockstar San Diego Employees" wrote a public letter alleging harsh twelve-hour-a-day, six-day-a-week workweeks during the development of *Red Dead* and *Midnight Club: Los Angeles*. Rockstar's labor practices, they wrote, had "turned [employees] into machines as they are slowly robbed of their humanity." The group pursued a class-action case with more than 100 employees, which Rockstar eventually settled out of court for $2.75 million. In a lot of ways, the company's grueling development process haunts the game: the inescapable feeling that such scope, such complexity, and such detail was achieved at so great a human cost. As usual, the ironic gap between Rockstar's anti-authoritarian sensibility and decidedly authoritarian company policies resulted in a game that poses many questions—about power, coercion, and what it would mean for a massive authority to give a life of dignity to someone in its charge—that are worth posing to Rockstar itself.

Before and after *Red Dead*'s release, fans and critics called it "Grand Theft Horse"—and they weren't wrong. Built on the same engine that runs Rockstar's 2008 blockbuster *Grand Theft Auto IV*, *Red Dead* borrows many design elements from the GTA series—the GPS system, the control scheme (press Y to steal car/horse), the "Wanted" meter that gradually drains down while you're evading lawmen—and offers a similar buffet of anarchic possibilities. Like GTA, it pads out its central narrative by making you run lots of errands for major characters, some of whom are noble and goodhearted (e.g. Bonnie MacFarlane) and most of whom are corrupt and flamboyantly degenerate. It also dots the landscape with "Stranger" missions in which specialized NPCs ask you to do even weirder stuff: expose an affair, rescue a mule, pick flowers for a woman who turns up dead. As critic Simon Parkin wrote in his Eurogamer review of *Red Dead*, "Liberty City with its buffed taxis, resolute skyscrapers and air of affluence may appear a world away from this arid, adverse wilderness, but peel back the skin and the framework is identical." Marston can feel at times like the true soulmate of Niko Bellic, the protagonist of *GTA4*, an immigrant who seeks his own kind of redemption in America and never quite shakes off the weight of his inescapable past.

Yet in many ways the game also transcends its sister series, and even props up GTA as an implicit, offscreen foil. The storytelling is more sober, the writing more restrained and less interested in taking cheap, Bill Maher-esque potshots at the excesses of 21st century American culture. The game gains many of its surprising thrills from reining in GTA's excesses. *Red Dead* has a wanted system, but it's necessarily less robust in an early 20th century world, and therefore easier to manipulate: At its highest level you end up avoiding

U.S. Marshals rather than helicopters and tanks. You can buy your way out of a bounty more easily than you can escape justice in GTA—but because of that difference, you can see just how little the Law has jurisdiction over the land you traverse, and acts of violence feel more decisive and consequential. Memories of Rockstar's metropolises make the rural landscape feel more open yet also, somehow, more claustrophobic, since there's nowhere to hide. Like any good Western, *Red Dead* gains some of its gravitas from leaving the petty world of city folk behind.

If the game had to pick another literary genre, it would be tragedy. Aristotle proposed that tragic heroes are tragic because they bring about their own fall, despite having good intentions. Check. He insisted that tragic heroes should be neither angels nor demons, absolutely good nor absolutely evil, since it's easier to identify with people in the middle. Check: Marston has an "Honor" meter that ticks up when he saves a kidnapped damsel on the side of the road, and ticks down when he steals a horse. (There's also a Fame meter that increases when you do anything of note, regardless of its moral tilt.) In the main story, he has a moral compass that tends to guide him toward doing the right thing; it also, sometimes, doesn't. Aristotle thought that tragedies are effective because they provoke a catharsis in the audience, an upwelling of pity and fear that stems from our vicarious involvement in the hero's pain. Few games are capable of eliciting pity as much as *Red Dead*—pity for the imprisonment of a man who seemed so free. Even the way the world of the game ends up becoming GTA by the end—when you reach the city of Blackwater and there are policemen on every corner, motorcars in the streets, gun peddlers selling automatic weapons—feels like a tragedy on a larger scale.

But the game's tragic mood depends entirely on the way it yokes together two other genres: the Western on the one hand, and the open world game on the other, a kind of third-person action game predicated on the idea of roaming around a freely explorable map. At first glance, the formula makes perfect sense, and it's almost surprising no other game (except *Red Dead 2*) has tried to pull it off. Both the Western and the open world game imagine freedom, or at least the illusion of freedom. Both privilege the horizontal expanse. Both take place in frontier lands full of vulnerable people and brittle institutions that can be exploited, destroyed, or saved. Both ask us to invest ourselves—as viewers, as players—in the figure of a wandering hero whose morality is an open question. The Western delivered these tropes to generations of 20th century moviegoers; the open world game invites contemporary players to inhabit them. That it has become the dominant genre of big-budget videogames—becoming almost an ur-genre underpinning games of every kind—shows us the enduring appeal, maybe even the necessity, of the ideas encoded in its form. Like any pop culture artifact, movies and games are like dreams; they reflect our fears and desires back at us. Genres are even larger dreams, dreams on a mass scale, constantly repeating themselves, that show us the fears and desires that undergird our collective thinking. The 20th century wanted the Western. We want the open world. *Red Dead* can show us how, in so many ways, they're more or less the same thing.

Yet they're also not the same thing at all. The open world is a design philosophy, determining what players can do, what kind of virtual space they can inhabit, and what counts as winning. The Western is a collection of images, tropes, and storytelling conventions from a long and evolving history of revisions and self-erasures. The open world can only improve; the Western has the power to undermine itself, to interrogate and expose its own basic assumptions. This is what makes *Red Dead* a uniquely powerful genre hodgepodge: the way its narrative fits its gameplay like a long, inescapable shadow; the way one half meets the other in a duel on an empty street. The way its Westernness plunges the very concept of the open world into a deeper history of longing—and a deeper history of ideas about what America really is.

Rockstar's method has always been essentially akin to collage. Guided by the college-dorm-film-buff tastes of the Houser brothers, they create games that splice together the ideas, story beats, and aesthetic touchstones of major American film genres. *Red Dead* is no different. It's a true mosaic, pulling bits and pieces from every stage of the Western's long history. Marston is a cowboy with a little of everything: the dirty taciturnity of Clint Eastwood, the plainspoken decency of Henry Fonda, the weary reluctance of Gary Cooper, the charismatic nihilism of Bonnie and Clyde. The "West" he lives in, postcard-perfect at every turn, is a collage of deeply familiar settings: John Ford's Monument Valley vistas; Sergio Leone's wild Mexico; the intricate one-street towns immortalized in movies and shows like *My Darling Clementine* and *Deadwood*. Members of the development team have been candid (for Rockstar, at least) about their desire to evoke the darker, revisionist Westerns of the 60s and 70s—movies like *The Wild Bunch*, *Unforgiven*, *High Plains Drifter*, and *The Proposition*; novels by Cormac McCarthy—rather than the heroic and jingoistic John Wayne oaters that came earlier. As lead designer Christian Cantamessa explained in a post-release interview, "Our overarching theme is the 'Death of the West' rather than the more conventional 'Myth of the West.'" Even so, he acknowledged that "all the classic Western moments, scenes you remember from years of films and television" were fair game for the team to transform into gameplay; their aim was to deliver "a complete Western experience."

If the game's voracious ingestion of the genre makes it feel rich and alive, it also leaves it saddled with complicated baggage. For the Western has never been just a form of entertainment. As the film critic J. Hoberman wrote in a 1991 essay eulogizing a genre that has never died, for most of the 20th century the Western was the "vehicle America used to explain itself to itself." No other film genre is as deeply intertwined with the shifting trajectories of American history—as an expression of them, an attempt to grapple with them, and an influence on them—than the Western. No other genre is as inextricably intertwined with the evolution of American taste.

To our 21st century eyes, the Western is quaint. It's a creaky antique that doesn't seem capable of existing on its own anymore without being massively transformed—either into an ultraviolent, ultra-nasty version of itself (like *The Hateful Eight*), or into one of several ingredients in a multi-genre sandwich (like *Westworld*). But for much of the 20th century, the Western was a dominant form. It didn't just stand on its own; it towered above other genres, forming a major part of the motion-picture diet of American audiences. As the French film critic Andre Bazin pointed out in the early 50s, some of the earliest experiments in motion-picture technology depicted Western themes, making the Western perhaps "the only genre whose origins are almost identical with those of the cinema itself." That inherent connection between the medium of film and a certain stable of image—cacti, gunfights, solitary rangers against the stark, dusty landscape—only deepened in the decades to come. "From roughly 1900 to 1975 a significant portion of the adolescent male population spent every Saturday afternoon at the movies," writes Jane Tompkins in *West of Everything*, her philosophical study of the genre. "What they saw there were Westerns." In this span of time, Hollywood pumped out hundreds of Western films and dozens of Western radio shows. In 1959, more than 30 Westerns aired on TV simultaneously. Some of these shows, including *Gunsmoke* and *Bonanza*, rank among the longest-running television shows of all time. "In one way or another," Tompkins writes, "Westerns touched the lives of virtually everyone who lived during the first three-quarters of this century." They touched the lives of American citizens across the socioeconomic spectrum. The Greatest Generation, the Silent Generation, the Boomers—all were raised on Westerns, which deeply affected the way they viewed the nation in which they lived and the wars in which they would inevitably participate.

The Western also touched the lives of immigrants—people from elsewhere who looked to the Western for an image of the American promise. And what they found in it was not necessarily a desirable setting (there's nothing about the desert that screams "You should move here!"), but, rather, a desirable image of the American self, the American character: what being an American entailed. My grandfather was an Italian immigrant, and he loved John Wayne. My wife's grandfather was a Cuban exile, and he loved John Wayne, too. And John Wayne wasn't the only one: Gary Cooper, Clint Eastwood, Jimmy Stewart, and Henry Fonda were all potent American icons. Even Ronald Reagan would ascend to the position of an actual American figurehead partly on the strength of his iconicity as a cowboy hero.

I never loved John Wayne. Nor did I grow up loving the Western. The first time I saw Wayne onscreen was in a high school film class presided over by an old left-winger named Mr. Loose, who had made it his multi-decade crusade to reprogram the unexamined politics of the tri-state area's Irish-, German-, and Italian-American boys. We watched *The Searchers*, John Ford's 1956 epic about a grizzled Civil War vet (Wayne) who goes on a quest to rescue his niece from Comanches. Mr. Loose taught us a new term, "miscegenation," and showed us how the film spoke to a fear of mixing the races, of losing a grip on white racial purity.

My dad mostly hated the Western, too. He was an inveterate city-dweller who had fled Argentina in the 70s because the military junta was hunting down and "disappearing" Communists. He had no taste for American exceptionalism and tended to look at it from a position of anthropological detachment. I grew up hearing him call George W. Bush, our Stetson-wearing cowboy president, a "caveman warmonger" who was stoking the bloodlust of the rubes. And yet he came from a country with its own cowboy traditions, the *gauchos*, and he cherished the memory of a time he rode down into the Grand Canyon on the back of a hapless donkey. He loved horses, and horseback riding had been a huge part of the life he had lived before me. A residual attachment to that world—to the world of animals and the dramas of the soil—was one of the reasons he hated the video games I played growing up. But he couldn't look away when I showed him a new game with a cowboy at the center of the screen, galloping, with a real sense of weight, into sun-soaked plains of endless space. Years later he would still refer to it as "that game with the horse."

"That game with the horse." I remember the way my dad would say it almost wistfully, as if *Red Dead* were one of the only games capable of depicting something true. For him the game tapped into something primal, in spite of its modern medium. What it tapped into is the core appeal of the Western as a whole. It's easy to think, as I once thought, that the appeal of the Western resides solely in the way it shows certain kinds of white men exactly what they want to see. Tough, broad-shouldered masculinity. American exceptionalism. A triumphalist and racist narrative of American history in which, through subjugating nature and the natives, our fledgling nation prevails. A nostalgic, idealized past in which old-fashioned values—honor, duty, justice—are threatened by the city and its ills. But not all Westerns feature these things, even if many of them do; the genre is capacious, ideologically flexible. What unites *all* Westerns, according to Tompkins, is the way they bring you to a certain kind of place. That place is brutal: a place of hardship and pain under the unforgiving sun. A place plagued by all manner of crime and injustice: rape, murder, thievery, racism, genocide. A place ruled and overshadowed by two forces in alignment: death and the natural landscape, neither of which cares who your daddy is or where you went to school. A place that feels real because it's so close to the ground—and feels fake because it's so obviously a soundstage, built for cheap and simple thrills.

But that simplicity might be its most important feature. The Western brings us to a place that, for all its horizontal expansiveness, feels bounded and legible in a way the city can never be. As the film critic Robert

Warshow put it in his 1954 essay "Movie Chronicle: The Westerner," "The Western presents itself as being without mystery, its whole universe comprehended in what we see on the screen." There's a scene in *A Fistful of Dollars* when Clint Eastwood's Man with No Name climbs to the balcony of the local saloon and takes in the entire town of San Miguel—a town that resembles *Red Dead*'s Chuparosa—with one panoramic survey. There are two gangs. One is headquartered here; the other is headquartered there. One is running liquor; the other is running guns. Both are rotten, both have to die, but between them lies a broken nuclear family—a husband, a child, and a wife, kidnapped and separated—that Eastwood takes it upon himself to reconstruct. In John Ford's *Stagecoach*, a movie so crisp that Bazin once described it as "like a wheel [...] [that] remains in equilibrium on its axis in any position," a group of passengers all crammed into the same coach end up forming a little microcosm of society at large, like Chaucer's *The Canterbury Tales*: there's the genteel Southerner, the crooked banker, the pure-hearted prostitute, the honor-bound cowboy (played, of course, by John Wayne). Even *Red Dead*, despite the hugeness of its world, has a scale limited by its genre; as Parkin observed in his review, "the borders of your missions expand at a slow pace, hour by hour, ensuring you grow familiar with the dirt paths and settlements and begin to build a memory map of the world and its sights."

In a way, the Western does what much sci-fi does: It transplants contemporary problems to a space removed from the messiness of the present—in this case the past, not the future—in order to imagine them with the clarity of distance. H.G. Wells's *The Time Machine* (1895), one of the oldest forerunners of modern sci-fi, addressed rampant class inequality in late-Victorian Britain by imagining a far-future in which the different classes—the ethereal Eloi and the brutish Morlocks—have become different species. In the 60s, *Star Trek* tackled civil rights by using aliens to talk about race. Even now, HBO's *Westworld* has remained committed to examining the existential vexations of a world governed by big data through the grandiose metaphor of a theme park in which the real and the fake cannot be distinguished, and the harvested data of park guests is "the product."

But the Western doesn't have any of the cold intellectualism of sci-fi, or any of the argumentative specificity. It feels instead like myth: an imaginative space in which even larger ideas, problems, and conflicts can be personified. The screenwriter Philip Yordan, who wrote a number of big Westerns in the 50s (including *The Man from Laramie* and *Johnny Guitar*), once said that he wanted to use the Western to "find again the purities of heroes of ancient tragedies." The impulse is understandable: America doesn't have ancient tragedies of its own, nor does it have a founding epic. We don't have our own King Arthur, Achilles, or Aeneas; our nation is too young. We've always had the Western, though: a genre in which figures representing different values, institutions, and political ideas can duke it out. A genre that can depict the beginning of things, prehistoric and primeval—even if it tends to represent a relatively brief and problematic phase in American history, long postdating the founding of the republic. In *Horizons West*, his study of the Western, the film critic Jim Kitses calls them "shifting antimonies"—the basic conflicts that Westerns depict, time and time again. Freedom vs. restriction. Integrity vs. compromise. Purity vs. corruption. Tradition vs. change. The individual vs. the community. Nature vs. culture. The West vs. the East. The definitions of these terms change from film to film; the conflicts always return.

Red Dead has that mythic simplicity—that austerity of vision that makes it feel, sometimes, like allegory. Part of its simplicity is intrinsic to the nature of the medium: Games always take place at an abstracted remove from the real world, in a bounded space defined by rules, binary conflicts, and constraint. But the game is also simple in its own way, in a Western way, especially compared to the sprawl of GTA. It has a stable of characters who personify different forces: cutthroat G-men who stand in for the encroachment of state power; a retired cowboy, Landon Ricketts, who represents a code of honor from a bygone era; a cocaine-addled anthropologist, Harold MacDougal, who embodies all the delusions and insecurities of 19th century racism. It has a hero caught between antimonies at every turn: humans vs. nature; law vs. lawlessness; honor vs. dishonor; the old way vs. the new regime. It has a tragic plot arc that depends, like all tragedy, on a story of limited scope. And above all, it has the basic tensions between its aesthetic genre and its gameplay—between the open world game, which stresses freedom, and the Western, which ceaselessly asks what freedom really entails.

Hoberman argued that the Western was America's way of talking to itself about itself because it could dramatize fundamental questions: "Who makes the law? What is the order? Where is the frontier? Which ones are the good guys? Why is it that a man's gotta do what a man's gotta do—and how does he do it?" By inviting players into the Western's elemental world, *Red Dead* raises questions of a similar kind. In the figure of Marston—and what you do as him—it raises questions about masculinity, cowboy heroism, and whether a person can escape their past. In its gameplay, it raises questions about death and the nature of violence and the attractions of physicality in an age of digital illusions. In the way it depicts American history, it raises questions about the brutal cost of "progress," the efficacy of political action, and the agency of the individual. In the way it depicts the West as a whole, it raises questions about what we want from that world, and what might be lacking in the world we already inhabit. It raises some of these questions deliberately, through the familiar mechanisms of satire; Rockstar games have always held up a funhouse mirror to "America," and this one is no different. But it raises larger questions whether it wants to or not, simply by hitching its horse to a wagon train that stretches back into the recesses of America's collective unconscious. What makes it a compelling game is the way it forces you to think critically about the dreams it embodies: the dream of the Western, the dream of the frontier, and the dream of the open world itself.

TERRITORY

CLOSE YOUR EYES AND PICTURE A WESTERN. What kind of place do you see? It might be the saloon, with its worn, half-size double doors, an out-of-tune player piano, and the threat of violence simmering under revelry. It might be the open street outside—a general store, a Chinese laundry, a barbershop/dentist—where horsemen kick up dust and tumbleweeds lope by. Or maybe what you see is Monument Valley, with its bluffs and buttes and impossible mesas, sticking out of the ground like the fat fingers of a rocky titan. No matter what, it will be a place tied to a certain kind of landscape.

That landscape is horizontal. Ridiculously horizontal. It stretches out in every direction, to the end of the earth and beyond, promising freedom, opportunity, and escape. As the great 18th-century essayist Joseph Addison wrote, "A spacious horizon is an Image of Liberty." Eternal expansiveness implies infinite possibility: There's always a place, on the remote horizon, where you can go next. But this expansiveness is also terrifying. It's sublime in the way that huge, craggy European mountains—the mountains in Romantic paintings—are sublime, except for the opposite reasons. It instills awe and terror not because it's shrouded but because it's empty. What you see is what you get.

Look out at that landscape. Not only do you have nowhere to hide; you can plainly see the kind of destruction that awaits you, and how difficult it would be to gain any kind of control over the vast, unforgiving waste. At the beginning of *The Mill on the Floss*, George Eliot's 1862 novel, the narrator salivates over a lush, verdant British landscape and says something deeply strange: "I am in love with moistness." The Western is in love with dryness—with an environment that has been leeched of life. An environment "inimical to human beings," as Tompkins points out, where the only things that live are hard, bitter creatures like vultures, coyotes, and prickly cacti.

And yet, there's something about that uninhabitability that is appealing in its own way. Something about it exerts an indescribable pull. On the one hand, it promises an encounter with the unconquerable, the last remaining place where humans have not gone. On the other hand, it promises pain: a refining, purgatorial toil that singes off the self's unnecessary encrustations, a return to the basic materials of existence. "From dust you were made, and to dust you shall return," the Bible tells us. The Western's landscape promises that return. Which is another way of saying it promises death.

Red Dead Redemption announces its obsession with the landscape from the very first moment you turn on the game. The title screen opens a long, thin window onto a portion of it, cropped in a way that evokes both the Super Panavision vistas of the genre and Sergio Leone's close-ups of squinting eyes. Cropping is a way of framing things that emphasizes reduction: nothing unnecessary, everything boiled down to the essentials. *Red Dead* tells us right away that it isn't going to be stuffed with crap. It isn't going to be like Grand Theft Auto, engorged with people and activities and radio stations and constant noise. It will be simple. It will be austere. It will be the kind of narrative that the Western is famous for, a story of elemental conflict between humans, death, and the landscape that always serves as death's willing accomplice.

But the title screen also changes every time you boot up the game, showing us different parts of the game's world. Snow-capped mountains and marshy swamps. Bustling storefronts and dilapidated barns. The morning light filtering through a thicket of narrow pines. The game announces both the simplicity and the *diversity* of its world, which is divided into three huge and very different zones: New Austin, Nuevo Paraíso, and West Elizabeth. Each area has a different feel, each is suffused with a wholly different set of cultural signifiers, and each turns the game into a different kind of Western. Marston's always up against something, but the nature of the enemy changes from place to place.

New Austin

New Austin, the game's first area, is also the area that feels most like a frontier. It's habitable, if barely: green trees and yellowing grass shade the landscape of Hennigan's Stead, where Bonnie MacFarlane ekes out a semi-prosperous existence grazing cattle on semi-dry fields. The game illuminates the fragility of the life her father built out here—the life she continues to nurture like a struggling baby plant. Bonnie's ranch is under constant threat, both from wildlife and from roving bandits. Late in her mission sequence, you come back with her to find the barn blazing, in a scene that evokes the blazing homestead in John Ford's *The Searchers*.

Of course, Bonnie's ranch feels like an idyll compared to other places in this region. To descend the steep cliff that closes off Hennigan's Stead, dividing it from a valley called Cholla Springs and other places farther west, is to descend into arid wastes all the more steeped in conflict and compromise. Soon after you leave Bonnie's ranch for the first time, you come upon Armadillo, the game's most prototypical Western boomtown. Armadillo feels like Tombstone in *My Darling Clementine*, or Sweetwater in *Westworld*: the kind of place where you never get lost and could easily come to learn everybody's business. Main Street, the only street, features an undertaker, a bank, a doctor, a barber/dentist, a gunsmith, a saloon, a sheriff's office, and a general store. The storefronts reflect the parsimonious lives of the people who use them—the town has nothing more than the bare necessities. Then again, the different architecture of different places might tell us more: The gunsmith and the saloon are grandiose two-story buildings while the sheriff's office is a collapsing shack, where a little NPC will occasionally come and get water from a sad, rusty pump. True to its namesake, Armadillo feels bounded, safe in its simplicity. But it's also creeping with danger, in part because it sits in the middle of the valley, totally exposed to the surrounding elements—naked, almost, as if the backs of its buildings were the inviting flesh of helpless cattle. There's nowhere to hide. Stand in the middle of Main Street and a gang will blaze through before long. The Marshal struggles not necessarily to keep order, but to maintain a brittle equilibrium.

The farther west you go, the more desolate the territory becomes. In the mission "Hanging Bonnie MacFarlane," Bonnie is being held hostage by bandits in a distant ghost town named Tumbleweed, and you head there to rescue her. The volumetric light is really something during this ride into the sunset—blinding and confrontational, yet strangely enveloping. You ride into it with a sense of urgency befitting a Western hero. And yet by the time you reach Tumbleweed, it becomes clear that the town's greatest threat might be capitalism, which has reached out from the East like a set of long, spindly tentacles and terraformed the land. Tumbleweed is its victim, a corpse created by the railroad company's capricious decision to build a station in Armadillo. In many Westerns the promise of economic nourishment is brought to some places and denied others, by a nameless and faceless abstraction over which citizens have zero control. In *Johnny Guitar* and *Once Upon a Time in the West*, people lose their lives trying to obtain, and defend, the tiny slice of land where a station might be built. No such bloodshed occurs in *Red Dead*; it's 1911, far too late. But it's still early enough for enterprising latecomers to seize a chunk of the world to come, through wiles or bribery or plain, old-fashioned killing.

New Austin is a place steeped in what historian Richard Slotkin calls the "unremitting puritanism" of pioneer life. In every little corner of the map you find either the elect—stern, driven people, exemplars of the Protestant work ethic, struggling to carve a better life for themselves, or the damned—degenerate hucksters with neither inhibitions nor compunctions.

In the former camp is someone like Bonnie, a second-generation pioneer. It was her father, the original settler, who subdued the land and the Indians; now it's her turn to fight off "white trash." Here's the thing, though: "white trash" is Rockstar's bread and butter (think Trevor in *GTA5*). You interact with the damned, not the elect, much more frequently: the reprobates, the parasites, the fast-talking con men. There's Nigel West Dickens, the quack who tries and fails to peddle snake oil to an unsuspecting populace. There's the simply-named "Irish," who boozes and lies and cheats. And then there's Seth Briars, the most degenerate of them all—a sort of cross between Gollum and Harry Dean Stanton whom you can often find exhuming corpses outside Coot's Chapel. The chapel stands imperiously, undaunted, evoking that "unremitting puritanism." Like the wooden chapel in *There Will Be Blood*, Coot's Chapel conjures images of the fire of an angry God being preached to a previous generation—a generation that needed promises to justify their own pain. But it's derelict now, used only by unsavory NPCs who sit in the pews, or visit the graves, and cry. The graveyard includes graves for all five of Bonnie's dead brothers. New Austin can be cruel in the way it mocks the elect and favors the damned.

Nuevo Paraíso

If New Austin is Puritan, then Nuevo Paraíso—the game's second zone and *Red Dead*'s version of Mexico—is Catholic, both in its embrace of Catholic iconography (the cross, the Virgin, the saints) and in its decadent obsessions with death and the suffering body. Like Dante, Marston descends into a kind of Hell that mocks the pretensions of the world of the living. Sepulcro ("tomb") lies in the middle of Perdido ("lost"), which is the middle part of the country: at the center of everything, an over-crowded cemetery, bristling with crosses. To the west lies Las Hermanas, an impressive Spanish-style convent, and probably the largest building in the whole region aside from the governor's palace. The main storyline doesn't involve the nuns who live at Las Hermanas, but the game invites you to bring your rambunctious, gun-toting self into their little simulacrum of a sacred space. If you're a good enough person, according to the game's morality meter, one of them might come out and give you a rosary that weakens the accuracy of your enemies.

To the west of the convent lies Chuparosa ("rose sucker"), a town roughly the size of Armadillo that feels like its melodramatic shadow. *Red Dead*'s "Mexico" is drawn from many Westerns, but most vividly from Sergio Leone's "Man with No Name" trilogy (*A Fistful of Dollars*, *For a Few Dollars More*, and *The Good, the Bad, and the Ugly*), films with a heavy Catholic atmosphere that makes shootouts and standoffs feel almost like rites performed in a profane desert mass. Like San Miguel, the village in *A Fistful of Dollars*, Chuparosa is full of whitewashed buildings and a lone cantina, anchored by a two-story *alcalde* that looks like the bottom half of a skull. Bad things tend to happen in the streets of Armadillo, but *nothing* good can happen here.

As Tompkins has pointed out, the Western's penchant for spectacles of pain and thirst and self-denial is much older than its American subject matter. It goes back to images and stories of saints who sought martyrdom in the harsh terrain of the desert. The medieval church was obsessed with desert saints, holding them up as icons of an absolute asceticism that mere monks could never match. In his *Confessions*, St. Augustine yearns for the moral clarity of St. Antony of Egypt, a hermit who spent decades living alone in the desert outside Alexandria. Centuries later, the Victorians would become obsessed with desert saints as well, in a way that had a few things in common with the American fixation on cowboys. In an era of increasing capital, consumerism, and urban expansion, the image of someone so reduced—deprived of water and denied comfort, with skin turned leathery by the penetrating sun—commanded an exotic appeal. Alfred Tennyson's 1842 poem "Saint Simeon Stylites" describes one of the most famous of these figures: a saint who is said to have spent 37 years living atop a narrow pillar of rock in the desert outside Aleppo. Told from the saint's perspective, the poem is a monologue that carefully accounts for all the pains and pestilences he has experienced. Yet it also has a sneaky way of questioning the moral purity of its subject:

> Let this avail, just, dreadful, mighty God,
>
> This not be all in vain, that thrice ten years,
>
> Thrice multiplied by superhuman pangs,
>
> In hungers and in thirsts, fevers and cold,
>
> In coughs, aches, stitches, ulcerous throes and cramps,
>
> A sign betwixt the meadow and the cloud,
>
> Patient on this tall pillar I have borne
>
> Rain, wind, frost, heat, hail, damp, and sleet, and snow;

Tennyson's St. Simeon harbors some ugly feelings: a perverse pride in the rough life he has weathered, and an *expectation* that God will grant him deliverance just because has suffered so much. The pillar is almost an image of the thin precipice between self-denial and self-indulgence: At what point does one become the other? At what point does suffering—gratuitous suffering—cease to be the road to salvation?

Red Dead's Mexico, like Sergio Leone's, raises these questions, often through ironic contrasts between the place's saintly aura and its battalions of degenerate sinners. *The Good, the Bad, and the Ugly* contains a scene in which the Ugly, Tuco, stumbles into the monastery where his brother lives and knocks a bunch of saint statues to the floor. He tends to make the sign of the cross before killing somebody. "Where we came from," he says, "you either become a priest or a bandit." A late *Red Dead* mission finds Marston being led by agents of the Mexican government—Captain de Santa and his men—into a local church, where he's been told he will find the two outlaws he seeks. For a second, from his point of view, we see the murals of the saints that frame the humble altar. Images of suffering, images of the saved. The "Redemption" in the game's title feels like a loaded word here—maybe with meaning, probably with mockery.

In Diez Coronas to the east, an arid no man's land full of massive mesas jutting into the sky, *Red Dead* presents its own pillars for wannabe St. Simeons to set up shop. The landscape evokes Monument Valley, a real-world part of the Colorado Plateau near the Arizona-Utah border that became deeply associated with the Western in cultural memory after appearing in the films of John Ford. In *Stagecoach*, in *My Darling Clementine*, in *The Searchers*, everything happens against the backdrop of these terra-cotta-orange mammoths, and everything feels small as a consequence. In black and white, they're imposing. In color, they're mythic, towering over the tiny silhouettes of the riders that ride beneath. Strangely and interestingly, however, Rockstar chose to put Monument Valley in "Mexico," not America. The decision has consequences. No zone in the game is more interested in undercutting the significance, impact, and self-importance of human affairs than Nuevo Paraíso. Primordial and unchanging, the rocks overshadow the political violence that takes place beneath them. An old Spanish fort named Torquemada sits on a steep rock outcropping among the mesas. Its battered walls have seen hundreds of years of conflict, but it looks like a Lego set against the backdrop of prehistory. In a similar way, the geology—the sheer verticality—of the region dwarfs the tiny shack where Luisa and her family are trying to live, as if their hopes and dreams for change, for justice, form only a little encrustation on the titan's timeless back. The music in Nuevo Paraíso reflects this fatalism, mourning the land with the plaintive notes of muffled mariachi trumpets. They rise tepidly into fanfare, but they always slump back down.

Such fatalism can easily slide into gallows humor, which explains why *Red Dead*'s Mexico is also, at times, its funniest realm. *A Fistful of Dollars* mines a lot of comedy from the figure of the coffin-maker, the only man in town with a reliable stream of income. In *Red Dead's* Mexico, mordant bits of humor like this proliferate. A random saloon in the wilderness: five caballeros ride by, shooting the air and cackling with glee while they drag a tied-up gentleman behind them. You will often encounter a man trying, and failing, to drag his donkey across the road: "Ya basta, burrito! Ándale, rápido!" So many of the Spanish names of things are jokes— maybe at the expense of non-speakers (like Marston), but maybe also as a way for the speakers themselves to memorialize their hardship and despair. It's tempting to say this is just a Rockstar thing; in GTA games, a lot of the satire resides in what things are called. Then again, almost none of the English place names in *Red Dead* are as loaded—or, sometimes, as ironic—as the Spanish ones. Torquemada was an Inquisition torturer. Roca de Madera means "rock of wood." Nosalida means "no exit." Punta Orgullo means "point [of] pride." And even Escalera ("stairway"), with its huge ramp *up* to the governor's palace, is a kind of merciless joke: Is there any hope of raising this place from the injustices that keep it down?

West Elizabeth

The game's final area is also its most compact and fragmentary. We find, in close proximity, three extremely different places: the snow-capped mountains of Tall Trees on one side, embodying nature in its most unremitting brutality; the bustling city of Blackwater on the other, embodying civilization at its most refined; and in the middle, the Great Plains, a space of gorgeous vistas suffused with the promise of free land. These places coexist uneasily, and each is also riven with deep and intractable self-contradictions. All three represent ideals from the history of American images; all three show that there is no ideal without a steep and visible price.

A deep "Main Street, U.S.A." vibe permeates Blackwater, the game's burgeoning metropolis. To stand in the middle of town—to look down the barrel of its main drag, past the electric lights, past the cafes and shop windows, all the way to the spire of City Hall—is to feel the hopeful grandiosity of a small place that believes in its own future. It's the kind of place that Walt Disney immortalized many times in his obsession with the kind of "progress" embodied by small-town America: a planned town, almost utopian, designed on rational principles and fueled by the irrepressible spirit of American entrepreneurship. But if it wants to convey progress, it also wants to convey age and permanence and stature. On one side of the town square is a squat, imposing Neoclassical bank with columns made of stone. It's the kind of bank that will form the cornerstone of 20th century economic life in many cities across the United States, representing the durability and trustworthiness of established institutions. That is, at least until the deregulated, postmodern finance capitalism of the 90s and 2000s will come along and let everything solid melt into air (a phenomenon satirized by the volatile stock market in *Grand Theft Auto V*). It's the kind of bank that, in any Western, not only begs to be robbed but ends up providing a strange kind of catharsis when it *is* robbed. The money is tangible. The inequality is tangible, too, and therefore reparable in a way it isn't in our own era, when the idea of robbing a bank has become a quaint anachronism. In New York City, the ruins of old banks like this are everywhere; most have become a CVS or a Duane Reade.

The urban design of Blackwater also cribs earnestly from the great metropolises of late-19th-century Europe. The Blackwater Grand Theatre is an eminent Victorian edifice, as stately as the bank, with huge chandeliers, velvety upholstery, and sweeping staircases in the lobby. Other imports from Europe suggest more of a mix of tradition and modernization—the Old World that was reinventing itself under the light of gas lamps. Blackwater's Main Street is designed like a Parisian boulevard, built wide to accommodate automobile traffic and flanked at the corners by outdoor cafes. The Blackwater Saloon features an ornate wrought-iron patio that evokes the Paris arcades—a detail that suggests not just decadence, not just luxury, but also an embrace of the urbanism to come. (*Red Dead 2*'s Saint Denis, an enormous riff on New Orleans, makes the Continental aspirations of Blackwater look quaint by comparison.) Then again, some architectural elements in Blackwater still yearn for a certain kind of past. Enclosed by two stories of white-picket railing, the Althewaye Inn is like Thieves' Landing, the game's swampy, Louisiana-ish hideaway for gamblers and crooks: a small piece of Dixieland that reminds us that the modernizing West will never quite shake some of core values of the antebellum South.

If most of these buildings have an ironic underside, the whole town has one, too: Blackwater's Main Street, U.S.A. is also, like the one in each of Disney's theme parks, a self-conscious front, a quaint, charming facade propped up by the much less savory forms of commerce that lurk behind it. The next street over, by the water-front, is the city's real main drag, featuring a gunsmith, a coffin-maker, a Chinese laundry, and a butcher with sliced-open pig carcasses hanging in the wind. Signifiers of hard work and rude frontier living abound: a shop for "Tools Fixtures Lumber & Nails," with a clothesline swaying over it; stores with cowboy paraphernalia like R.J. Dutton Tack & Feed; ramshackle wooden buildings. The streets around Main Street allow us to see that in a previous generation this place was another Armadillo, a pop-up city on the fringe, and it still hasn't shaken the vestiges of its birth. All the new toys—the bank, the theatre, the candy store on Main Street—are still being paid off through violence and bloody opportunism. The blood is just elsewhere now, pushed to another margin.

If anything, the most truly developed part of the whole place is its police force, centering on a huge station in the northeastern part of the city where The Bureau, a proto-FBI, has its headquarters. Bowler-hatted policemen patrol the streets, constantly reminding the player that, as Rockstar's Dan Houser put it in an interview with IGN, the game depicts a "movement" from a situation of "violent freedom" to "[a] situation of much more overt state control." In both *Grand Theft Auto IV* and *V*, you start off by helping out small-time crooks and end up working on behalf of the biggest crooks of all: the federal government. *Red Dead* presents the same basic, satirical trajectory, but wraps it in a much more depressing sense of cyclicality and inevitability. Marston is never not working for the U.S. government, which feels a lot stranger and more claustrophobic in a place still bathed in the signifiers of individual freedom and opportunity (unlike GTA's super-developed Liberty City or Los Santos).

Tall Trees, the game's mountainous Ozarks region, represents the place where Marston might be able to escape. Tall Trees is Blackwater's negative image, the last bastion of natural forces opposing the unstoppable encroachment of East-Coast "civilization." In Tall Trees, no matter how much hardware you're carrying, you can still be mauled to death by a bear or gored by a wild boar. The cold light shimmers on the river as it winds its way through rocks and bluffs.

In Tall Trees, the game becomes a Snow Western, tapping into a history of images that emerged alongside—and sometimes in tension with—the usual desert tropes. In the same way that some video games have an ice level, some Westerns (for example, *The Searchers* and *Django Unchained*) have snow sequences, where the hero faces new and wholly different natural obstacles. Other Westerns (*The Track of the Cat*, *Johnny Guitar*, *The Hateful Eight*) take place exclusively in wintry environments, using the setting to explore a different kind of solitude, a different kind of relationship between self and world. Or a different kind of death. Agoraphobia becomes claustrophobia. The wandering ronin on the wide plains becomes the hermit in a cabin, berated by the elements. The corpse dried by the sun and eaten by buzzards becomes the corpse mangled by bears, encased in ice.

Red Dead 2 begins as a Snow Western, crystallizing the elemental conflict between humans and nature, warmth vs. the unremitting cold, in the contrast between the dim orange glow of protagonist Arthur Morgan's lantern and the blizzard that swirls around him. But it might be more fitting that Marston heads into Tall Trees at the end of the game, because the Snow Western more traditionally depicts the end of the line—the last remaining pocket of true, unconquered wilderness after all other spaces (including the desert) have been colonized. In *Jeremiah Johnson* (1971), a young Robert Redford heads into the snowy mountains on an *Into the Wild*-style quest to abandon civilization. He has no idea where he's going; he just wants to keep heading "due West" until he finds a place where "there's beaver to trap." What he finds instead, minutes into the film, is a pretty clear reason to stop what he's doing and just go home. He sees a body frozen in the ice, with a note attached:

> I, Hatchet Jack, being of sound mind and broken legs, do hereby leave my bear rifle to whoever finds it. Lord hope it be a white man. It is a good rifle, and killed the bear that killed me. Anyway, I am dead.
>
> Yours truly,
>
> Hatchet Jack

Hatchet Jack anticipates one of the most common tropes of "environmental storytelling" in big-budget video games: the dead body lying next to a darkly comic note. Like the carefully laid-out corpses in *Fallout* and *Bioshock*, Jack even provides Jeremiah with a pretty serious weapon upgrade.

But the joke of the film is not just that Jeremiah is terrible at being a mountain man, or even that being a mountain man is a terrible idea. The joke is that no place in the mountains is truly uninhabited; his dream of virgin land is ironized from the start by the people who live there already. First, he meets lunatic hermits who have been rendered almost as inhuman as their surroundings, one of whom laughs maniacally while being pursued by a bear. But he also meets Native Americans who have used the frigid zone as their final retreat from genocide. And it's this part of the film that resonates most acutely with *Red Dead*, because Tall Trees is never really the place where Marston goes to confront nature. It's the place where he goes to confront his other life—where Dutch van der Linde has holed up with his gang of Native Americans, and where Marston ends up slaughtering them en masse.

There are two ways to read the game's representation of Native Americans. On the one hand, you could read the fact that they appear almost exclusively as part of Dutch's gang as a crafty way of excusing their genocide at Marston's hand, which is a strategy aligned with the Western's broader forms of erasure. So many Westerns throughout the history of the genre have retroactively justified and whitewashed genocide by depicting "Indians" as hooting savages. So many more have made that genocide easier to swallow not even by painting them as monstrous enemies, but by relegating them to the backdrop—pretending they don't exist. In a revealing passage in *West of Everything*, Tompkins describes the horrible realization that most of the Westerns she'd seen (besides outliers like *Dances with Wolves*) hadn't even bothered representing Native Americans at all except as a vague, abstract threat, compounding their historical erasure with a representational one.

If you wanted to be more charitable, however, you could also read *Red Dead's* representation of Native Americans as another kind of dark satire. Maybe the game is trying to show that in this place where, as Bonnie MacFarlane says, the previous generation—her father's generation—completely decimated the Indians, all that's left for them is a life of criminality on the margins of society under a neo-feudal gang lord. The game pushes us toward this interpretation through the sympathetic and tragic character of Nastas, a Native American who serves as quack anthropologist Harold MacDougal's taciturn sidekick, and ends up dead after trying to broker a pow-wow between some of the gang members and his idiotic racist associate. The whole exchange between MacDougal, Nastas, and the members of Dutch's gang is worth quoting:

MacDougal: Hello, gentlemen. We come in peace!

Native American: Those words mean nothing coming from people like you. Look at what you have done to us, look at us! We live like animals, scrambling in the dirt.

MacDougal: Well I…I…violence isn't the answer.

Native American: Maybe you live in a different America than we.

MacDougal: Men like Van der Linde will lead you to disaster.

Native American: I think we've already experienced disaster. The likes which you could only imagine. Put your hands up!

MacDougal: We come in peace! [whispering] Do as he says, Marston!

Marston: You call this a meeting?

Native American 2: Give me your damn weaponry!

Nastas: This is not what we agreed.

Native American: You shut your mouth, you treacherous snake.

[Native American shoots Nastas in the face.]

It's hard to decide how to read a scene like this, or a character like Nastas. But there is something horribly, tragically fitting about the way the game forces you, as Marston—another marginalized figure, another outcast, another enemy of the state—to be responsible for the final eradication of the Native American presence in this land.

And so we come to the Great Plains, a region that seems to exist mostly as backdrop—the horizontal vista at the edge of Tall Trees's verticality, the amber waves of grain fueling Blackwater's crass expansionism. It's a region as perfectly composed as the landscape paintings of the Hudson River School, suggesting—with each carriage under the sun, with each solitary horseman under the stars—a harmony between humans and nature. The song "Home on the Range" bears the same promise:

> Oh give me a home where the buffalo roam,
>
> Where the deer and the antelope play,
>
> Where seldom is heard a discouraging word,
>
> And the skies are not cloudy all day.

But the people at Rockstar can be clever satirists, and the Great Plains contain ironies just as bitter as those that define Tall Trees and Blackwater. You can admire your home where the buffalo roam; you can also exterminate all twenty of them, permanently, to get an achievement called "Manifest Destiny." As a joke, the achievement is a little on-the-nose, but it also reminds us of the fragility of a space like this, already carved up by telephone lines.

It also reminds us of the fragility of Marston's home, a ranch called Beecher's Hope. The name ironically evokes pre-Civil War abolitionist and clergyman Henry Ward Beecher, embodying a desire for freedom that will forever be forestalled. The place itself is saturated with that and more—a sense of middle-class aspiration, of hard-won individualism eked out from the harsh and bitter soil. Inside: three bedrooms, a piano, a kitchen table, a Tiffany lamp in the corner, rugs in almost every room, covering up the raw timber. Outside: a barn, a corn silo, plenty of land. After Marston returns home from his tribulations, things get back to normal for a time. He helps Abby, Jack, and Uncle—an inept, drunken lout who knew him from his gang days, another symbol of the tenacious grip of the past—with mundane tasks. You buy cattle, hunt elk, round up horses. The game often forces you to spend the night before doing these tasks, asking you to adopt the regularity of domestic life rather than the inhuman sleeplessness of adventure. You can sometimes see Abby washing the windows outside the house. Preservation, rather than destruction, becomes your purpose in this place.

But every task you undertake to preserve Beecher's Hope feels overshadowed by a looming sense of futility, vulnerability, and impermanence. Abby and John have set down roots, but their tree is still a sapling, and bulldozers are on the horizon. In one mission, Abby asks you to take care of a cloud of black crows swarming around the corn silo. You pick them off, one at a time, and defend it in the short term, but their numbers are incalculable, and you know they'll always come back. I've never played another game in which an entire mission functioned as a metaphor, a grim omen of events yet to come, but this one does. It portends the fact that Marston's reinsertion into the home will be tragically short-lived: the same barn he worked so hard to build will become the place where a troop of soldiers and federal agents fill his body with bullets. His previous life catches up to him; any redemption represented by the home becomes impossible. The game, like *The Odyssey*, depicts a homecoming—*nostos*, a Greek word at the root of *nostalgia*—only to ask whether homecoming is truly possible for its wandering hero. Or whether humanity is possible for a hero who has spent so much time doing inhuman things.

There's a small and possibly unintentional joke built into Beecher's Hope: a treasure chest in the attic. Open it up and you'll find $20—not bad when you adjust for inflation. But it's a chest that really asks you to ask yourself: What the hell are you doing? Are you stealing from yourself? Has the acquisitive logic of *Red Dead's* open-world gameplay left you unable to do anything but *take*—even from the family you worked so hard to return to? In a similar way, John's last few missions are boring, but they might be deliberately so. They seem designed to foreground the fundamental incompatibility of gameplay and everyday life. Life at home is selfless and other-oriented rather than self-interested and solipsistic. Life at home is about building things, giving, and staying rooted, rather than destroying things, taking, and moving on.

Beecher's Hope allows you to imagine another way of living—another way of playing *Red Dead*—that is poignantly impossible. In this respect, it's like no other place in the game. But in another respect, it *is* like other places in the way it's filled with a dark potential energy, balanced on a knife's edge between life and death, hope and despair. The haystacks will become cover, the corn silo will become a sniping point, the barn will become one last refuge. The farm will become a battlefield, erupting into chaos. But then it will become a farm again—just as Armadillo will forget its daily skirmishes and Nuevo Paraíso will forget its revolution. In the Western, violence doesn't destroy a place. It is quickly and unceremoniously metabolized.

FRONTIER

I DON'T LIVE IN ANY of the places evoked by *Red Dead Redemption*. A year ago, I moved to Miami, an urban, tropical, distinctly modern setting that Rockstar already recreated in *GTA: Vice City*, which is a very different game. But in coming to know this southernmost slice of the United States—this piece of the South that isn't the South at all—I've come to realize that the logic of the West is buried here, too. Like the farthest-flung Western territories, Southern Florida was mostly uninhabited until Henry Flagler's East Coast Railway cut into it in 1896. Even then, it would take decades to tame under the heel of progress. People literally traveled around the area by boat, winding through mangrove tunnels like Venetians among the gators. A onetime Union soldier named Dr. Horace Porter established a U.S. Post Office for "Cocoanut Grove" in 1873, giving the area of Miami its name; he left soon after and it was forgotten, consumed by the tireless jungle. But the rawness of the place is exactly what attracted certain types of people from the Northeast to set up shop. Homesteaders, eccentrics, bootleggers, utopians. Some of them rich, some of them poor, some of them brilliant, some of them fools.

The area is home to so many vestiges of wild, quixotic projects. I'm thinking of Monkey Jungle, a primate utopia "Where Humans Are Caged and Monkeys Run Wild!" that was established by a renegade animal behaviorist in 1935. I'm thinking of the Miami Serpentarium, a roadside snake-lover's fantasia where an obsessive herpetologist named Bill Haast spent decades conducting experiments that involved poisoning himself with venom. I'm thinking of Vizcaya, the obscenely huge estate of early-20th century industrialist James Deering, a villa in the jungle with every nook and cranny filled with gold and marble and priceless art—and even Coral Gables, which was an attempt by one man, George Merrick, to make his own version of Spain.

But most of all I'm thinking of a man named Edward Leedskalnin, a tiny Latvian immigrant who moved to a plot of land in southern Dade County and spent several decades building a complex of buildings and statues out of gigantic coral rocks. He apparently built the "Coral Castle" (also known as "Florida's Stonehenge") himself, moving the ten-ton blocks of coral with an improvised system of pulleys and levers, but supernatural speculations—aliens, the Illuminati, secret magnet powers—haunt the place.

My wife and I call it "One Man's Dream"—the strange yet apparently universal truth that nearly every significant tourist attraction in Florida is the remnant of some early-20th- century megalomaniac's quasi-utopian passion project (including the biggest "One Man's Dream" of all, Disney World). I find myself inspired by these tales of pioneers who trudged into a hostile environment and shaped it into something original and personal, like Leedskalnin's coral sculptures. I also find myself wary of the way such verve can represent the other side of a dark and merciless ego—a violent hatred for others, masquerading as eccentricity. In the gift shop at Coral Castle you can buy Leedskalnin's book, which, as it turns out, isn't a manual on how to move coral but a psychotic and deeply misogynist screed against girls who get "soiled" before marriage.

The frontier beckons. Sometimes it beckons the good. Sometimes it beckons the foolish. Sometimes it beckons the egos who hunger for territory, grabbing slices of the world to fill a hole in their rotten souls.

You find all three in *Red Dead*. The question is, which one are you going to be?

•

What kind of game is *Red Dead*? You wouldn't be wrong if you said it's a video game that plays like every other big-budget, single-player game that has hit the market in the last ten years. Like *Breath of the Wild*, the Arkham games, *Shadow of Mordor*, *The Witcher 3*, the Tomb Raider reboots, the *God of War* reboot, *Horizon Zero Dawn*, *Final Fantasy XV*, the *Assassin's Creed* series… the list goes on and on, *Red Dead* is an open-world, third-person character action game that takes place on a freely explorable map. If you disregard the third-person part, it shares elements with even more games that have graced the shelves of your local GameStop: the Far Cry series, modern Fallout, The Elder Scrolls.

Although they vary in the details, these games all follow a similar script. You roam from place to place. You probably climb some sort of tower. You kill bunches of enemies that spawn in the open wilderness. You ride from story mission to story mission, each of which takes you to a different part of the realm. And you do activities, clearly demarcated by little icons on the map: sidequests, bandit outposts, treasure hunts, animal hunts, people hunts, races, card games, rescue missions, robberies. *Red Dead* has all of these; so does *The Witcher 3*; so does GTA; so does *Assassin's Creed Origins*.

If *Red Dead* plays like other games, it's not necessarily because it belongs to the same genre, but rather because it fits neatly into the overall design philosophy that has creeped into the vast majority of big-budget video game titles over the last decade. It fits into a category of video game that the AV Club's Clayton Purdom has usefully termed the "map game." The map game "isn't so much a genre," Purdom writes, "as it is an overriding philosophy on what makes games fun, an epochal undercurrent. It's a constant drip-feed of XP and an endless checklist of collectibles and activities, all varied slightly by their set dressings and a mechanic or two." Most big-budget single-player games are map games now.

In a map game, you *pretend* to inhabit the vast, intricately designed world that surrounds you on all sides. But in practice, what you really do is live on the map screen, with its clean informational overlay and its activity icons telling you calmly, insistently, where you should direct your attention next. For some people—like my brother-in-law, a professional completionist who collected all 900 Korok seeds in *Breath of the Wild*—the collectibles, XP, and activities instill a drive to do everything. I suspect that for most people, like myself, the mountain of tasks is less exciting than it is, in a strange way, reassuring. You will always have stuff to do, and none of it will be particularly high-stakes. The genre ensures a steady, ceaseless dopamine drip of busywork.

Map games don't begin that way, though. They begin with wonder. They begin with the promising exoticism of a new place, a new time, a new world with different rules of engagement than the real world. It's no accident that most Assassin's Creed games begin by asking you to ascend to some sort of vantage point, from which you can see the open world sprawling out in every direction. "We're meant to feel awe at the scope of creation," writes game critic Cameron Kunzelman. "Like looking at the Grand Canyon, we're supposed to be enthralled by the scale. We're supposed to think about how this wide work could swallow us up." We're supposed to yearn to escape into this digital vastness, where the finitudes of real life no longer apply.

And yet, somehow, seeing the vastness of the simulation also makes you want to smoosh it down to size. The great panorama makes you want to climb back down into the details: to do everything, go everywhere, experience all that there is to experience. It inflames the innate human desire for explanation—some of us may remember when "See those mountains? You can go there!" was a ubiquitous video game selling point. But the desire for exploration can slide easily into rapacious, acquisitive, crypto-colonialist feelings: an urge to conquer every corner of the world, to relentlessly and expansively territorialize. And these games do little to stem that urge. In many map games, reaching a vantage point will make a dozen activity icons spill onto the map like a bag of loose change. You descend from the tower, or the mountaintop, and care little for standing around and feeling the texture of the world. You blaze through it on a really fast horse, going from quest marker to quest marker, abusing the parkour system or some other larger-than-life movement mechanic to create a ridiculous beeline path to your destination. You clamber through clay houses and market stalls and shove your way through crowds of people. You kill who you need to kill, do what you need to do. You move on, not really having seen any of the spaces you blazed through, but with a sense nonetheless that you've taken more of the world as your own.

Over the course of the game, through endless iterations of this process, the world does indeed become your own. But it also becomes homogenized. Everything that was once new and strange becomes familiar, known, like a landmark on your daily commute. It's the ennui of tourism in general: the difference between when you first arrive in a place and when you feel, only a day or so later, that you're "done," ready to move on. You've seen the museums and the gardens, all the authentic places. You've eaten at a hole in the wall without any TripAdvisor reviews. You've added a notch to your belt, a Lonely Planet to your bookshelf. But you also feel nothing—maybe worse than nothing. In his 2004 essay "Consider the Lobster," David Foster Wallace describes the existential misery of being a modern tourist:

> To be a mass tourist, for me, is to become a pure late-date American: alien, ignorant, greedy for something you cannot ever have, disappointed

in a way you can never admit. It is to spoil, by way of sheer ontology, the very unspoiledness you are there to experience. It is to impose yourself on places that in all non-economic ways would be better, realer, without you.

The map game generates a version of this feeling, both because any game is going to be smaller and more conquerable than a real-world location, and because the logic of conquest itself—"doing" Paris, the Pyramids, Rome, Hong Kong—is intrinsic to the experience. The difference is that you're not really entering and despoiling a real place that would be better off without you; you're entering and despoiling a virtual place that was actually made *for* you. As game critic Will Partin has pointed out, the experience of playing something like *Watch Dogs 2*, with its steady drip of algorithmically generated incidents that pop up around the player based on his or her playing habits, is less like going to Paris and more like being fattened up on a cruise ship—an experience that Wallace describes in another essay ("A Supposedly Fun Thing I'll Never Do Again") that anticipates the banalities of the modern map game. What is a map game, if not, as Wallace says of cruise ships, a "blend of relaxation and stimulation, stressless indulgence and frantic tourism, that special mix of servility and condescension that's marketed under configurations of the verb 'to pamper'"?

And yet the selling point of open world games isn't pampering at all. It's the promise of the frontier. That feeling of excitement when you see the wide world spread out around you, that desire to escape into it, to live in a space of expansiveness and freedom: this is a desire *for* the frontier. And the desire to live on the frontier goes hand in hand with a desire to seize a piece of it for yourself—to better your condition (as our nation once "bettered" its own condition) through territorial expansion. Open world games almost always take place in frontier spaces of one kind or another—either truly new and unexplored territories (see *No Man's Sky*, with its procedurally generated galaxies), or, more commonly, familiar spaces *rendered* new by post-apocalypse or some other form of defamiliarization. *Fallout 3*'s Washington, DC is a frontier; *The Division*'s New York City is a frontier; *Assassin's Creed IV*'s Caribbean is explicitly a version of the Caribbean where treasure is still buried, where islands can be claimed, and where Nassau is a frontier city that can become a pirate utopia. Even *Grand Theft Auto V*'s contemporary Los Angeles is a frontier because it presents a version of our own LA with fewer people and without as much order, still ripe for the economic taking. In these games, as in the original promise of the frontier, progress and territorial expansion are intertwined. You know you've made it, as a player, when your map screen shows that the outposts have been captured, the territories have been subdued, and the activities have been completed. When you know the West was won.

This equation of progress with territorial expansion is an idea lodged deeply in America's collective unconscious. For several decades, it was understood by many historians to be the story of America itself. In 1893, the historian Frederick Jackson Turner delivered "The Significance of the Frontier in American History," a keynote address to the World's Columbian Exposition in which he argued that up until that point, the frontier had been the driving force behind America's progress as a nation. He argued not just that the United States had developed socially and economically through its westward expansion, but also that the nation's peculiar character—its penchant for self-reliance, self-reinvention, individualism, and the new—had been forged in its travails along "the meeting point between savagery and civilization." The frontier was a space to be won, in Turner's estimation. And in the winning of it, America itself had emerged and evolved.

Historians of the Western have often remarked upon the weird—or maybe fitting—coincidence that Turner delivered this address only blocks away from one of Buffalo Bill's Wild West Shows, an over-the-top, hootin' and hollerin' spectacle of lasso tricks and reenacted skirmishes between staged cowboys and Indians. It was a fortuitous coincidence because Westerns themselves are rich and often complicated expressions of Turner's thesis. Sometimes they celebrate the frontier; sometimes they mourn it. Sometimes they celebrate "progress"; sometimes they reject it. In either case, they tend to equate the development of the United States with the conquering of the wilderness and the subjugation of the land, which they also tend to allegorize through the individual struggles of their protagonists. In *How the West Was Won*, an epic 1962 Western projected in super-widescreen using the Cinerama process (which involved three projectors working in sync to make a huge, curved image), one family's multi-generational journey from New York to California becomes an allegory for the growth of America itself from a hardscrabble frontier territory into a technological superpower. A series of dissolves at the end of the film show the red, Mars-like terrain of the desert transforming into civilization. Arid craters become lush agricultural fields. A dam fills a valley of death with lifegiving, man-made water. Endless sand gives way to the apex of enlightenment: a network of modern, bustling freeways.

Red Dead vividly demonstrates how the logic of the frontier is built into the structure of open-world gameplay. In one moment, you're travelling into a vast, open landscape—a land beckoning you into its emptiness. In the next moment, you're killing the people who are already there, dropping entire platoons with quick lever-like pulls of the left and right trigger. These activities are not tonally or conceptually mismatched, as they often are in games (e.g. *Uncharted*) that try to graft shooting sequences onto exploration. Instead, they're intertwined: systematic murder often lurks on the other side of "exploration," and exploration is presented as a task never quite finished without systematic murder. *Red Dead* uses its own open-world formula—in which roaming and machine-like slaughter necessitate each other like two parts of a rhyming couplet—to embody, rather than simply depict, the history of violent expansionism that Westerns often celebrate.

Why does the market crave these games? Why do *we* crave them? Maybe because we've gone even further beyond the "closing" of the frontier that Turner lamented. The globalized world we live in has rendered frontiers impossible. John F. Kennedy anticipated this development when he named outer space the "New Frontier" in his acceptance speech at the 1960 Democratic National Convention, in LA:

> I stand tonight facing west on what was once the last frontier. From the lands that stretch 3000 miles behind me, the pioneers of old gave up their

safety, their comfort and sometimes their lives to build a new world here in the West [...] [But] the problems are not all solved and the battles are not all won, and we stand today on the edge of a New Frontier—the frontier of the 1960s, a frontier of unknown opportunities and paths, a frontier of unfulfilled hopes and threats[.] [...] For the harsh facts of the matter are that we stand on this frontier at a turning point in history.

Kennedy's rhetoric gives us one way to think about the rise of sci-fi, which supplanted the Western as a dominant American cultural genre after the 1980s. But his speech also embodies the darker prospect that there are no more worlds to conquer. Or the idea that, as the environmental philosopher Jedediah Purdy has put it, there is no more empty space, free space, beyond the "built world that sustains us"—a world in which "for every pound of an average person's body, there are 30 tons of infrastructure: roads, houses, sidewalks, utility grids, intensively farmed soil, and so forth." A world in which "there really is no more outside." Open world games are built to help us escape from this oppressive, cramped reality. It's too bad that most of them inevitably make it worse by revealing that they're for *you*. They're cheap, pandering simulations of freedom. They're outgrowths of the infrastructure state.

Breath of the Wild is an incredibly vast game with many features that try to resist this depressing irony. Hyrule is new again, enigmatic and fresh, a realm full of unmarked secrets and recalcitrant details. The map contains few icons at all—certainly none telling you the kinds of activities you can do. Even so, I remember vividly the moment I came to the northern edge of the map and felt the game's finitude. Once I saw the edge, the boundary, Hyrule was irreparably demystified. The bigger the world, the harder it falls into disenchantment.

Yet some examples of the genre really do resist disenchantment. What makes map games *work*? They work when they put you in the shoes of a protagonist who has a better reason to wander around than you do—someone whose relationship to the world isn't about tourism, consumption, or conquest. One example is Geralt of Rivia in *The Witcher 3*, an itinerant monster-hunter who often has a complicated relationship to the communities that hire him. On the one hand, they need him. On the other hand, they hate him: Like an exiled ronin, he experiences a potent combination of fame and alienation as he travels from village to village. In *The Witcher 3*, character and setting shape each other in an endless feedback loop: If Geralt were not Geralt, the world would not seem so imposing, or so beautifully ugly, or so consumed with injustice. If the world were not this way, Geralt himself wouldn't be so impactful as a protagonist, so possessed of qualities that attract and repulse the player. The world doesn't feel like a place that's for you, or a level you can beat. It feels like an alien place, a broken place, that only someone as broken and as alien as Geralt can navigate.

So the open world game ends up being a paradox. The logic of the frontier might be hard-coded into the genre, but the best examples of the genre resist the logic of the frontier. They place you in the shoes not of an explorer who might conquer the new world, but of someone who has lived in the world already—someone who has history with it, who has been shaped by it, who will probably die in its grasp. John Marston is that kind of character, and the world he inhabits is that kind of world: not really a frontier at all, even if it looks like one in every way. Like *The Witcher 3*, which it undoubtedly influenced, *Red Dead* creates a feedback loop between character and world that resists the usual equation of "progress" (XP; skill trees; becoming better, faster, stronger) with territorial expansion. In a basic sense, you *do* get more stuff when you proceed through the story and unlock different zones of the game. But Marston also remains weirdly static, if not actively self-destructive. You don't feel like you're consuming the world. You feel like you're being consumed by it.

There is no XP system in *Red Dead Redemption*. There are no rewards—aside from a few dollars here and there—for killing more people than you need to kill, or for completing the activities that dot the landscape. There is no such thing as "winning." Marston begins the game as good as he'll ever be at shootouts (minus a few Dead Eye upgrades), and the lock-on system allows you to play the game without ever getting better. There are no levels. There are outposts to claim, but they don't really do anything. You can buy properties, but none of them have any real futurity; they're simply beds where a worn out gunfighter might lay his head to rest.

It's sort of astonishing to contemplate how much the game shuns the sense of progression that other games enshrine. In 8-bit platformers and roguelikes, you reset your progress every time you die, forcing you to start anew as a naked babe. But even *they* derive their replayability and their overall appeal from the feeling that you're getting a little better every time. You've become quicker; you've internalized the rhythm; you know how to cope with the multitudinous threats. 'Hardcore' games like *Dark Souls* and *Super Meat Boy* are about failure—histories of failure written in trails of blood. But you move on eventually, and you get better.

Red Dead mocks your progress. If anything, progress for Marston involves not an ascent into expertise but a descent into depravity—a moral cheapening. He doesn't avenge anything, doesn't pursue wealth or power. He doesn't even achieve atonement or a spiritual cleansing:

Any redemption he earns is only in the eyes of the state, and the state is corrupt. He does what he's gotta do because he's being coerced. He's a dog on a leash. There's an unpleasant stasis, a circularity, to his condition. If anything, the better you get at the game, the more it reminds you that you're becoming like the enemy—the machines that kill hundreds of men, or the government that has taken on the imperialist role usually inhabited by the open-world hero.

Or you're becoming capital-P "Progress" itself, which characters in the game complain about relentlessly. "Change is only good when it makes things better," Bonnie says. Her skepticism of Progress is common to the Western, where the real enemy is often not the desperado in a black bandana but the stuff that just got here: the railroad, the Federal government, the power of East Coast money. The genre wistfully venerates old ways and dying breeds. In this game, that skepticism of Progress, of the very idea of Progress, finds its voice not just in characters like Bonnie but in an almost pathological unwillingness to let Marston progress as a hero, or to let the player experience the kind of progression endemic to other games.

In the Western, writes Jane Tompkins, "the desert flatters the human figure by making it seem dominant and unique, dark against light, vertical against horizontal, solid against plane, detail against blankness."

Third-person open world games achieve a similar effect, offering players a sense of freedom against the constrained, knowledge against the benighted, capability against the inept, centrality against the peripheral. The player character stands tall in the middle of the frame, contrasting a teeming nation of bugs who swarm around him waiting to be swatted. You can flick the right analog stick and literally move the world around.

The open world game generates the fantasy that you are not *in* the world but on top of it, imposing your will upon it. But the world of *Red Dead* does its best to undercut the basic supremacy of this format. Marston is only ever a part of the world, and when the world gets trampled under the boots of progress, he gets trampled, too. What you move toward is not completion, not conquest, but self-annihilation—which seems fitting for a genre so obsessed with the inevitability that we will be defeated by the land we have tried to tame.

I have fond memories of one sidequest in *Red Dead* that is flagrantly, almost insultingly pointless. A man named Jeb Blankenship comes up to Marston and bluntly says, "Hey partner, I need your help." "You and every other fool around here," Marston responds—a good retort from an overworked Good Samaritan. Nevertheless, he decides to help the man, who is desperate for the return of "Jeb's girl." Marston assumes that Jeb's girl is his girlfriend, maybe his daughter. He rushes to Tumbleweed, where he fights off the hordes of bandits that have descended upon the ghost town like a swarm of maggots on a corpse. As it turns out, Jeb's girl is a horse. The mission simply ends with that punchline. You have wasted your time.

Open world games are seldom about dead ends, squandered potential, or wasted time; their design stresses limitlessness, both in terms of what the player can do and what the player can be. You can join every guild in *Skyrim*; you can keep sinking other ships in *Assassin's Creed IV: Black Flag* until you have over a billion reales and you're the seventh "Most Feared Pirate" on the North American leaderboard. (This is literally true of my father-in-law, who still plays the game, six years later, and views "pillaging and plundering" as an endless pastime best enjoyed in the hour before bed.) In the open world, you can keep progressing and progressing until the world has nothing and you have everything. You can't in *Red Dead*. You can own every gun, but it won't make Marston any more than himself, or the world any less hostile.

The frontier is a potent dream. That's why we keep dreaming it: in video games, in movies, in political rhetoric, in the collective unconscious of the American mind. *Red Dead* knows. But the game surrounds the freedom and endless accumulation of its genre—every killing spree, every algorithmically-generated skirmish, every property purchased, every animal slain—with a claustrophobic sense of encasement. All progression is stasis. All expansion erodes the soul. You can ride out to the edge of the world, but to reach it is to realize that you're trapped, like a *Westworld* guest, in an island prison built for you, with a control tower looming somewhere in the distance.

DEATH

YOU CAN TELL A LOT about a video game by the way
it depicts death. In *Dark Souls*, famously, your own
death is a constant spectacle: After hearing the telltale
shink of an enemy scythe or claw or hammer finally
getting the best of your pathetic avatar, you watch
yourself double over in pain, fall to your knees, and
finally keel over. The screen fades; the words "YOU
DIED" appear in huge and uncompromising capital
letters. Many games instead smooth over the face of
death, making it a seamless and unremarkable part of
your vicarious digital life. Death in *Uncharted* happens
all the time—as it should, given the suicidal jumps
Nathan Drake tries to pull off on a regular basis. But it's
as simple as a three-second fade to gray while Nathan
falls into the abyss, as his companion yells "Nathan!"
in momentary despair. Death in *Super Meat Boy* is
literally instantaneous; death in *Super Mario Bros.* is a
comic "oops" moment, with Mario facing the camera
in a pantomime of sweaty embarrassment.

Like *Dark Souls*, *Red Dead* wants you to know when you've died. Against a stark red background, it pastes the letters DEAD over Marston's mangled body. But the meaning of his death derives more from its particularity: No death is ever quite the same. Marston might tumble off his horse into the maw of a steep canyon. He might get shot in the knees, and then the shoulder, as he tries to find cover behind a dingy barrel. He might get mauled randomly, in the middle of nowhere, by a renegade cougar. Each death will look different because each will contort and batter the body in a different way—and the same goes for the thousands of enemies he kills. During one of the Nuevo Paraíso missions, the corrupt Federales contract Marston to exterminate rebels hiding out in a village called Tesoro Azul. I shot one of the rebels as he was climbing down a ladder. Even in death, the body still clung to the bottom rungs for three seconds before finally slumping off.

The distinctiveness of these deaths comes from Euphoria, a character behavior system that Rockstar has integrated into all their games since *Grand Theft Auto IV*. When you slam into the car in front of you in *GTA4* and your body smashes through the windshield—that's Euphoria. When you push someone down the subway stairs and their body slumps down each individual step with a grimly realistic sense of dead weight—that's Euphoria. When you shoot someone's leg in *Red Dead* and they clutch it in agony, limping while trying to fire back—that's Euphoria. The name, of course, feels more than a little ironic, given what the system does. Then again, it undeniably creates pleasure for the player by turning each death into a unique and flamboyant spectacle.

Originally developed by a six-person team at a company called NaturalMotion, Euphoria is less a physics engine than an extremely potent combination of animation and AI that sits on top of the physics engine, generating character behaviors on the fly in response to even the smallest bodily stimuli. From a development perspective, it's pretty expensive and inefficient. Euphoria generates a custom behavior every time a character's body interacts with the world in a certain way (e.g. when a character gets shot in the leg), which means that it is highly CPU-intensive. Because the nature of these behaviors will differ from game to game, it also needs to be programmed from scratch, bespoke, for every game that implements it. But the results might be worth it: The system creates an impressive level of detail, giving a heaviness to every fall and every footstep. Rockstar has been using and refining Euphoria for over a decade now, and it still forms a core component of their proprietary RAGE engine. According to Harry Denholm, former engineering lead at NaturalMotion, the company had *Red Dead* in mind—not *GTA4*—when they first became interested in Euphoria; *GTA4* only ended up coming out first because of a scheduling change.

It makes sense that they would have wanted to use Euphoria for a Western. First of all, it enabled Rockstar to capture the way people get shot in the Western—floridly, outrageously, tumbling off horses and over bars and down the staircases of bustling saloons. According to Christian Cantamessa, the game's lead designer, Euphoria allowed them to recreate "the classic 'stunt' falls of the most epic Westerns, where characters ride the momentum of a gunshot rather than fighting to remain upright." In another interview, the game's technical director, Ted Carson, made a similar point: "When colliding with the environment, the resulting reaction is not just physical, but performance-based—for example, glancing impacts with walls use true body mechanics to spin the character away, flip over a railing, fall down the stairs, get dragged by a horse, or whatever the environment calls for." Deaths in *Red Dead* are more "cinematic" than regular video game deaths. Each is a kind of silent movie in miniature.

Paradoxically, however, Euphoria also adds something that seems antithetical to this cinematic quality: a sense of realism. Deaths in *Red Dead* are not just florid; they are also brutal. As *Edge* magazine put it in their review of the game, "*GTAIV*'s modern weapons spit bullets like angry hornets until a health circle depletes; here, lives end in uncompromising fashion." Euphoria adds exactly the kind of realism Westerns strive for: one based in the tactility and fragility of the body, and the kinetic, unpredictable, often violent relationship between the body and the physical world. As Tompkins points out in *West of Everything*, "Physical sensations are the bedrock of the experience Westerns afford." She cites the first lines of *Hondo* (1953), a Western novel by Louis L'Amour: "He rolled the cigarette in his lips, liking the taste of the tobacco, squinting his eyes against the sun glare. His buckskin shirt, seasoned by sun, rain, and sweat, smelled stale and old."

The Western makes you hear the wheeze of a well-oiled revolver barrel, feel the creak of a wagon wheel over the dust-choked earth, see the hissing steam of a moving train. The Western lavishes attention on both objects and the basic logistical problems that objects can solve: Where am I going to get water? Where am I going to sleep? How do I get a rope around this thing? How long is it going to take to get from point A to point B, and will I die along the way? Depending on your mood, it can either remind you that you live in physical space or make you yearn for other spaces that are more physical than your own—the beach house where you got a splinter from driftwood, the cabin where your parents cooked under kerosene lamps. It satisfies a desire for the *real* that the contemporary world of shifting images so often refuses to give us. In *Red Dead*, these things are all-important. Stagecoaches bounce and tumble over the landscape in a way that makes you feel the weight and fragility of their component parts. Marston's lasso sails out and cinches around objects and bodies of various sizes as if every twine of it were separately animated; the rope really feels like a rope. In a post-release interview, Dan Houser speculated that a true Western game couldn't have existed before *Red Dead* because developers simply hadn't had the technology to "make horses, stagecoaches or rope—all vital aspects of a western experience—look or behave remotely sensibly." Ted Carson, Rockstar San Diego's technical director, echoed the sentiment: One of their top priorities as a developer was making "horses that felt right, lassos that behaved properly."

The irony, of course, is that the Western delivers this physicality through the immaterial medium of film, and *Red Dead*, even more ironically, delivers it through digital simulation—the very kind of thing that should make us yearn for physicality in the first place. Nevertheless, the Western pursues simple and pervasive reality effects, and always tries to express a lost and fundamentally physical authenticity. The genre gives us the real that resides in rope and wood and the smell of gunpowder in the morning. It draws its power from a deep fear that all we have are images, and that we've become estranged from our bodies, from the land, even from the overhanging threat of death. Video games are familiar with this fear. Like the

Western, they at once offer a salve for it, through their own attempts at tactility, and lock us deeper inside the house of mirrors we've built for ourselves. *Red Dead* is no different. Euphoria is one of the main technologies it uses to bring us into a world of palpable things.

And into a world of pain, too—pain and discomfort. In the Western, "most of the sensations the hero has are not pleasurable," writes Tompkins. "He is hot, tired, dirty, and thirsty much of the time; his muscles ache." Cormac McCarthy's dark, revisionist Western novel *Blood Meridian* begins with a vision of a child worn down to a little nub by the jagged landscape around him: "See the child. He is pale and thin, he wears a thin and ragged linen shirt. He stokes the scullery fire." As the child of the opening lines makes camp, McCarthy's style contracts into sentence fragments that simply tell us the things that surround him:

> A hole in the sand with rocks piled about it. A piece of dry hide for a cover and a stone to weight it down. There was a rawhide bucket with a rawhide bail and a rope of greasy leather. The bucket had a rock tied to the bail to help it tip and fill and he lowered it until the rope in his hand went slack while the mule watched over his shoulder.

The almost overwhelming tactility of the scene opens up a corridor of empathy between the child and the reader: We feel what he feels, vicariously but with unmistakable clarity. And what he feels is pain. None of these objects are smooth (except maybe the "greasy leather"); they press upon him, chafe his skin, weigh him down, scratch his body. They give him cover, but it's only thin protection from the penetrating elements. *Red Dead* strives for this kind of oppositional friction between bodies and objects. The game strives to make us feel how the world presses up against Marston—and how Marston presses back.

In Westerns, pain is the road to truth. Things feel real because the body needs them, whereas in the daily lives of the Western's presumptive viewers, things matter less and impress upon us less because we do not spend our days fighting for them. The Western doesn't aim to make us feel guilty about this comfort, however. If anything, it wants us to feel a little jealous—nostalgic for a world defined by different forms of self-making. In the East, in urban industrialized modernity, you make yourself by getting a job, making money, finding a partner, engaging in various rituals of social connection. In the mythic West of the Western, you make yourself by enduring toil. You prove what you have always *been*, deep down, by winning a contest of the flesh. You make yourself by using force and skill and violence to fend off the most literal forms of annihilation.

Red Dead is too easy to ever offer the player this kind of experience. The lock-on system, which snaps the target reticle to any nearby enemy with a quick pull of the left trigger, makes it too simple to kill people. Marston's automatic recovery from injuries— even if he can get injured very quickly—can't convey the vicissitudes of survival as effectively as something like *Metal Gear Solid 3*'s labor-intensive injury system, which forces you to bandage individual broken limbs. But the unique, Euphoria-generated reactions of the dying, and of Marston every time he dies, create the impression nevertheless of a place where the body is deeply exposed to physical vulnerability, and liable to be broken at any moment.

And the game creates other effects that heighten that impression even more, either through Euphoria or through its idiosyncratic control scheme. Marston never runs by default, like other video game protagonists who spend their entire waking lives jogging briskly through houses and towns. Instead, you have to prod him with the A button if you want him to go faster, in exactly the same way that you have to press A to get him to kick his horse. The control scheme creates a curious feeling of distance and indirectness: You don't always feel like you *are* him; instead, you feel like you're telling his body to do things, pulling the strings on a heavy and fleshy marionette. As you master the game, the sensation of indirectness—the feeling of delay between command and execution—gives way to a kind of practiced oneness. But this feeling of synchronization still feels more like riding a horse than driving a car: Even *Red Dead* experts will find that Marston's body has a mind of its own, a gravity of its own, that defies the player's control. His body remains a central part of the experience. And when Marston dies, you feel the destruction of that body in ways that other games seldom match. His deaths are often just as pathetic as the deaths of NPCs. He'll stagger back and collapse into the fetal position after getting bitten in the knee by a snake. He'll tumble off the side of a cliff and keep tumbling, tumbling, breaking every bone in his body as he tries in vain to grab onto something. Before the curtain draws and the word DEAD appears, the camera will zoom out a little and circle his limp frame, as if to emphasize its insignificance.

Any good Western is also a great, big *memento mori*: The genre wants to remind us that the body will die. In *Red Dead*, the reminder takes human shape in the form of the Strange Man, a pale, bowler-hatted gent who encounters Marston at several points. Likened by game critic Ed Smith to a "Shakespearean ghost," he always seems to know where Marston has been, who he's killed, and where he's eventually headed. "Ain't this a beautiful spot?" he says to Marston the last time they meet each other. They're standing at the spot where Marston, his wife Abigail, and their old companion, Uncle, will eventually be buried.

And yet, despite all the morbid pageantry of the Strange Man, the game's tumbling bodies and cumbersome gameplay convey a much less theatrical message. Like the Western, the most cinematic genre of all time, the game wants to remind us that death will not be cinematic; it will be small and humiliating and deeply physical. It will be, in the end, a matter of sheer matter, sheer logistics, and maybe even sheer chance, like a wagon wheel crunching over the belly of a hapless drunk. Or like a cowboy shot down in the middle of a town he barely knows, fighting for a cause he doesn't believe in, wondering when, if ever, his body will get to rest.

COWBOY

ON NOVEMBER 30, 2009, Rockstar released a trailer for *Red Dead* that introduced the world to John Marston. He's on his horse when we first see him, marching slowly, deliberately, across different swaths of the game's landscape, accompanied by the mournful trill of a jail-bird's harmonica. He marches across snowy mountains, craggy rocks, a sun-soaked prairie hill that frames him in silhouette against the sky. He marches into town, the hoofbeats of his horse matching the lethargic tempo of the men and women around him. And then, in a shot that frames just his rough gray pants and his spurs entering a doorway—a doorway that divides the blinding sun from the darkness within, unmistakably evoking John Wayne coming in from the wilderness at the beginning of *The Searchers*—he marches into a sheriff's office. "My name's John Marston," he says. "I'm here to capture or kill Bill Williamson." This version of Marston is all business, constantly in motion, with a steely determination in his eye. The trailer cuts between him robbing a train, aiming his rifle, riding solo through a valley that slices between impossibly steep plateaus. His voice never quavers; it remains the same confident monotone, dispensing soundbites that could only come from a seasoned, indestructible badass: "People don't forget. Nothing is forgiven."

The game itself doesn't give us that Marston. Or at least it doesn't give us that Marston without serious complications. In the trailer, he's gruff, imposing, larger-than-life. In the game he's slinky, almost Johnny Depp-like, cutting a narrow figure in the center of the screen that starkly contrasts the Ron Swanson bearishness of *Red Dead 2*'s Arthur Morgan. In the trailer he's proactive, starting fights and finishing what he started. In the game he's decidedly reactive; fights break out around him, fights he didn't want to get into, and he finds himself running from bullets as much as dispensing them. In the trailer, he seems to know exactly what he's doing; in the game, he has a naïve streak that leaves him beaten, broken, played. In the trailer his facial scars signify power; in the game they confess to his vulnerability. One of the first things that happens to him is a near-death experience: He marches right up to Fort Mercer, where Bill Williamson is holed up, and gets shot. In the trailer he transitions conspicuously from rags to riches, trading his roughed-up brown jacket and bandolier for a rakish suit and tie. In the game, you can make him rich, but you can't exactly make him successful—nor can you rescue him from an obscure, untimely, government-sanctioned death.

Marketing explains some of these discrepancies: The trailer wanted to cast a wide net, showing players the most badass possible version of the avatar they would inhabit. But these discrepancies also stem from Rockstar's complicated, ambivalent approach to the conventions of the cowboy, a figure that has been front-and-center in the pantheon of American cultural archetypes for over a century. Born amidst the racism and misogyny of the late 19th century, in an era of change where many prominent white men found solace in the idea of a new American Übermensch, the cowboy is a figure with a long history of ideological twists and turns. Like the Western itself, he has been subject to innumerable revisions and reimaginings. *Red Dead* understands that legacy and rejects much of it self-consciously, with every adulteration that makes Marston a figure of weakness and moral compromise. As it does in other ways, the game aligns itself with revisionist Westerns that dragged the cowboy down from his pedestal and ran him through the muck—movies that turned the cowboy into the much less shining image of the gunfighter. Yet the game also reveals just how hard it is to shake the ideas that have clung to the cowboy archetype from the very beginning—and just how much those ideas continue to shape our appetite for the figure at the center of American myth.

In the dark recesses of a 90s media cabinet, piled somewhere under the fat plastic cases of *Aladdin*, *The Little Mermaid*, *Beauty and the Beast*, and *The Land Before Time I-VI*, there's a Disney Sing-Along tape that my wife used to watch over and over again when she was a kid. The tape contains a song about cowboys that Disney produced sometime in the 1950s, when Walt's obsession with the West knew no bounds. The song is about the dream of a kid named Johnny, who lives in the big city yet has everything a cowboy needs. As the music lopes along, Johnny lopes along on his noble steed, transformed by an animator's pencil into the icon he yearns to be:

Oh, a cowboy needs a horse,

And he's gotta' have a rope,

And he oughta' have a song,

If he wants to keep ridin'.

The allure of the cowboy isn't quite as potent now as it was for the apple-cheeked 50s kids targeted by the song. But he remains with us, sometimes calling attention to his out-of-placeness in the postmodern world and sometimes making us yearn again for the world of simple, physical situations from which he hails. *Toy Story* wouldn't be *Toy Story* without Woody, whose old-fashioned values of honor and duty and self-sacrifice get him into trouble, yet always seem to end up correcting for the late-capitalist nihilism of their existences as throwaway commodities. *Overwatch* wouldn't be *Overwatch* without McCree, the (literal) straight shooter who keeps the game tethered both thematically and mechanically to more grounded forms of gunplay. *Red Dead* wouldn't be *Red Dead* without something similar: a figure at the center of the screen who can make us *feel* centered, inciting a strange and potent nostalgia. When I listened to the song, I thought of *Red Dead*'s trailer—the way it promises so earnestly that you, too, can become a cowboy, so long as you put on the right accessories. But then I thought of the game itself, and the way it's so tireless about questioning the appeal of the cowboy, even as it depends on his worn and familiar mystique. The game asks questions the song never bothers to ask: Who is the cowboy, anyway? Why would anyone want to be him?

•

It's tempting to trace the origin of the cowboy to the soup of 19th-century genres from which the Western itself emerged: stage melodramas; pulpy dime novels; the Leatherstocking novels of James Fenimore Cooper; the poetic romances of Henry Wadsworth Longfellow; endless reports of Wild West escapades that ran in Eastern newspapers and periodicals; Buffalo Bill's Wild West Shows, which toured the nation with dizzying spectacles of cowboy heroism from 1883 to 1913. And yet, as the game critic Reid McCarter has pointed out in his essay "*Red Dead Redemption* Never Escapes the Past," almost everything about the cowboy is older than that. The horse he rides, the cattle he herds—both were imported to the Americas by Spanish colonizers, and he himself is an import, too: "[T]he white, square-jawed cowboy is just one variation of a *vaquero* tradition dating back to Spain's medieval era, which itself stems from the horsemanship practiced by various Muslim countries which occupied the country as Moors." In his neo-chivalric code of honor and his wandering lifestyle, the cowboy also borrows elements from the ronin or the medieval knight-errant—a stranger from elsewhere, bound by a higher code. And yet the cowboy never really feels like an import, even if he has deep Old World roots. He appears to us fresh and free, unbound by any history except the days and nights of tiresome travel that are legible on his body.

It's hard to define what a cowboy is, but Tony Soprano (of all people) does a pretty good job. In the pilot episode of *The Sopranos*, the mob boss channels a whole deep history of immigrant aspiration when he complains to his new therapist, Dr. Melfi:

> Let me tell ya something. Nowadays, everybody's gotta go to shrinks, and counselors, and go on "Sally Jessy Raphael" and talk about their problems. What happened to Gary Cooper? The strong, silent type. That was an American. He wasn't in touch with his feelings. He just did what he had to do. See, what they didn't know was once they got Gary Cooper in touch with his feelings that they wouldn't be able to shut him up! And then it's dysfunction this, and dysfunction that, and dysfunction *vaffancul!*

Tony himself is an American archetype: a tortured, conflicted gangster antihero. But he's an archetype haunted by other archetypes to which he cannot help but feel inferior. Part of the problem is that he's a McMansion-dwelling suburbanite with obnoxious kids, late to the party that was the immigrant experience. Part of the problem is that Gary Cooper, the Cowboy with a capital-C, embodies a more detached relationship to violence. Tony might be a murderous sociopath, but he's still affected by violence in ways that he wishes he wasn't. It stalks his subconscious. For him to feel "un-American" because he needs therapy, because he can't just *kill*, tells us a lot about the kind of cultural and ideological messaging he and his father have absorbed from a century of Westerns. But the bigger problem for Tony is that the cowboy is more of a man than he is. The cowboy is an unattainable masculine ideal, bound inextricably to the definition of American virtue. No matter what Tony does, he'll never be able to be "the strong, silent type."

Tony's feelings about Gary Cooper echo the beginning of *The Virginian*, a 1902 novel by Owen Wister that gave the cowboy his shape as a quintessentially American icon. From the point of view of an onlooker from another world, we look upon the cowboy with envy. If that envy manifests for Tony as frustration and rage, however, it manifests for the narrator of *The Virginian* as something very different. He gets a good look at the Virginian and almost salivates:

> Lounging there at ease against the wall was a slim young giant, more beautiful than pictures. His broad, soft hat was pushed back; a loose-knotted, dull-scarlet handkerchief sagged from his throat, and one casual thumb was hooked in the cartridge-belt that slanted across his hips. He had plainly come many miles from somewhere

across the vast horizon, as the dust upon him showed. His boots were white with it. His overalls were gray with it. The weather-beaten bloom of his face shone through it duskily, as the ripe peaches look upon their trees in a dry season. But no dinginess of travel or shabbiness of attire could tarnish the splendor that radiated from his youth and strength. [...] Had I been [a] bride, I should have taken the giant, dust and all.

The description is over-the-top horny, revealing a pretty deep homoeroticism at the root of a genre often characterized—as video games in general are sometimes characterized—as a collection of power fantasies by and for straight men. The narrator doesn't just want to be the Virginian; he wants to be his "bride." Later on, he makes an even more explicit pronouncement: "Had I been a woman, it would have made me his to do what he pleased with on the spot."

What makes the cowboy so desirable? Partly his pure sense of style: a play of accessories and angles and relaxed-fit lines that flattens him into the cool unreality of a lifestyle advertisement. The way his "broad, soft hat was pushed back"; the way "one casual thumb was hooked in the cartridge-belt that slanted across his hips," in the same way the Marlboro Man reaches idly for the match in his denim-shirt pocket. In the same way that

Marston himself stands relaxed, his hat cocked down and his hands hooked softly into the pockets under his bandolier, while the viciously corrupt Coronel Allende yells and gesticulates about the savagery of the poor.

But an aura of effortlessness isn't the only thing that makes the cowboy alluring. What makes him desirable is also that he doesn't seem to desire anything—and seems, in fact, to be actively pursuing pain and discomfort, like an ascetic or a monk. His appearance opens a window into the pain of the body beneath. The Virginian "had plainly come many miles from somewhere across the vast horizon": a record of pain and endurance is written upon his figure. Yet he doesn't seem encumbered by it at all; just the opposite, he seems purified by it, as if having transcended pain is the source of his poise and equanimity. A purity shines through him even when he gets his hands dirty; he seems to have achieved contentment in the conditions of terminal, unending discontent.

The Virginian's appeal isn't about success. Gangsters strive for the aura of success, as Rockstar games have shown us many times. They claw their way to the big time—money, cars, real estate, power—in a twisted perversion of the American Dream. But the cowboy, as Robert Warshow pointed out in in his 1954 essay "Movie Chronicle: The Westerner," is a different kind of protagonist, standing oddly apart from the capital-ist logic of the society for which he is an icon. "The

Westerner is *par excellence* a man of leisure," writes Warshow. "Even when he wears the badge of a marshal or, more rarely, owns a ranch, he appears to be unemployed." He's at best underemployed, doing odd jobs at a leisurely pace. But it never bothers us that he doesn't seem interested in "getting ahead" like the gangster; if anything, his opposition to the drive of the gangster (and other capitalists) is his appeal: "Where could he want to 'get ahead' to? By the time we see him, he is already 'there': he can ride a horse faultlessly, keep his countenance in the face of death, and draw his gun a little faster and shoot it a little straighter than anyone he is likely to meet."

For what it's worth, the Virginian *does* end up rich by the end of Wister's novel, albeit reluctantly. Warshow's point stands, though, because it doesn't really matter. The allure of the cowboy isn't about money, fame, or even power, because that's what his opposite—the effete, metropolitan elite from the East Coast—already has. His allure is the fantasy of being reduced to basic, natural manhood.

Marston embodies these fantasies, too. Like the Virginian, he's a taciturn man who distrusts excessive verbiage and scorns the hucksters who tend to use it (and yet, at the same time, speaks in witty one-liners). Like the Virginian, he seems to possess not just a pseudo-Southern gentility but an inherent nobility, revealed through his contests with nature and criminals, which always justifies his violence against them. He always seems to stand apart, always seems to possess an incorruptible dignity, somehow refined—rather than corroded—by the undignified business of killing. He's a superhero—not just because he can see better than anybody, ride better than anybody, and nail six headshots from a mile away, but because he might be the only decent man in an indecent place.

But we can learn more about *Red Dead*'s version of the cowboy by taking a look at Marston's fans—the characters who are obsessed with him. One of the biggest is a Wister stand-in who appears in a series of Stranger sidequests: a hapless writer named Jimmy Saint who's come from Manhattan to "[capture] the spirit of the West for a monthly back East." The game ridicules Jimmy; he always needs to be rescued from gangs of bandits. And the game ridicules the way he looks at Marston:

> Jimmy: "My, my! Take a look at you. Will you take a look at you! You look like you've seen trouble, mister. Enough for a hundred men."

> Marston: "Trouble has a way of finding me, mister."

> Jimmy: "Do I like the sound of that? Do I ever like the sound of that."

Through the figure of Jimmy, *Red Dead* shows us how much it understands the original appeal of the cowboy as Wister imagined him: his style; his aura of self-denial and moral purity; his erotic allure to insecure metropolitan men. The way he's "seen trouble" that the East Coast man hasn't seen, crystallizing a purer kind of virtue that lies beneath a life of vice. But it's also striking how much the game wants to make that allure, that cowboy mystique, an object of irony and mockery. The fate of Jimmy is grim if you follow him to his ignoble end: After you're done with all four parts of his mission sequence, he will keep running across the landscape until he is attacked by a pack of 30-plus wolves.

Like Tony, and like the narrator of *The Virginian*, Jimmy makes one thing clear: The true appeal of the cowboy has a lot to do with the embittered, fragile masculinity of the men who imagine him. The late 19th and early 20th century were times of increasing empowerment and cultural visibility for women, and it's no coincidence that the "West" in the Western is a world where men control everything. As Tompkins points out, it's a world diametrically opposed to the domestic interiors of the 19th century novel, and created in reaction to them. Westerns privilege the outside over the inside, physical action over talk, isolation over social relationships. Spend a while peeling back their leathery macho surfaces and it becomes hard *not* to see the tremendous well of anger, insecurity, and entitlement—maybe even embarrassment—boiling beneath. If the cowboy is a hero, he's also a kind of monster, begat from those ugly feelings. Tompkins puts it bluntly: He embodies "men's fear of losing their mastery, and hence their identity, both of which the Western tirelessly reinvents."

To its credit, *Red Dead* displays an awareness of this problem. As game critic Jess Joho has noted, the game shows us that the true villain responsible for John's fall is not Bill Williamson, Dutch van der Linde, or even the government agents who execute him; "the blame rests squarely on the false promises of a world built on hypermasculine ideals." Scenes between John and his son, Jack, make this clear: Even though John tries to play the role of a caring and empathetic father, even though he tries to adopt a new model of masculinity, it's too little, too late; his son fixates on replicating all the macho, gunslinger bullshit. In one mission, it drives him to go fight a grizzly bear by himself: "I was trying to prove myself," he says to John; "You're always telling me that I read too many books. That I'm not a real man." It drives him to become what his father never wanted him to become: John Marston. The game's true ending occurs when, as Jack, you hunt down the man in charge of Marston's execution, Agent Edgar

Ross. He's retired now; you corner him at the edge of a river, where he's trying to catch some fish. Jack's bullet goes in his brain, and the game smash-cuts to the word "REDEMPTION" on a blood-red screen—one final, tragic irony. The cycle of violence begins again, greased and powered by male insecurity.

Male insecurity also shapes the game's depictions of women, though in a way that feels less intentional. You could argue that *Red Dead* deserves some credit for trying to avoid the violent misogyny of Grand Theft Auto, a series still known by many as "those games where you can hire and murder prostitutes." While every saloon in *Red Dead* has prostitutes, Marston can't hire any of them because he's a family man. Then again, as Joho points out, it's not exactly better that the game still encourages you to "hogtie a prostitute, put her on the back of your horse, and set her down on a train track as she screams for mercy before exploding under its wheels"—all for some notoriety points and an extremely dubious achievement. The larger problem with the game's female representation is encoded in that formula: No matter what Marston does to or with women, they exist to reflect back on him, either burnishing his honor (like when a nun appears out of Las Hermanas to give him a prize for his moral rectitude), revealing a dastardly streak, or otherwise lending him ever more shades of gray.

The game falls victim to a problem the Western has grappled with since the beginning of the genre: its inability to allow women to break out of stock types, or to extend to them the same level of moral complexity and existential self-conflict that the male heroes get to grapple with. Bonnie MacFarlane and Marston's wife, Abigail, the two major female characters in *Red Dead*, are both more complexly shaded than any of the female characters in GTA games. But they both cycle between types, never given the luxury of interiority or self-contradiction. They exist to illuminate Marston, and as a result they appear before us with a blinding, oversimplifying clarity. Bonnie starts off as the brash, self-sufficient cowgirl—a prototype for *Red Dead 2*'s Sadie Adler—but then becomes the damsel in distress. Abigail taps into a Western archetype even older than the Western itself, going back to the "soiled doves" of Victorian melodrama: the good prostitute who serves as a handmaiden to the redemption of her flawed, cowboy suitor. By the time we meet her, she's also become the nagging wife, there to remind Marston of his sins while highlighting everything that makes him cool. His flaws. His inner turmoil. His maleness.

But Marston's maleness is not the only thing that makes him appealing as a Western hero. To the disgraced anthropologist Harold MacDougal, he's also a paragon of whiteness. In the late mission "At Home with Dutch,"

MacDougal takes one look at Marston and fawns, like a good late-Victorian, over the man's racial stock:

> MacDougal: Tell me, sir, are you from Norse stock?

> Marston: Not as far as I know. I was raised in an orphanage. My father was Scottish.

> MacDougal: Unfortunate. You'd make an interesting case for my theory of natural population characteristics.

> Marston: Really?

> MacDougal: Why yes, a white man obviously, but, but, but with a savage spirit. Trust me, sir, I mean savage in the best possible sense. Natural nobility, but also simple. Pure.

With the phrase "natural nobility," Rockstar again reveals how much it understands something deep and pernicious buried in the "natural" appeal of the cowboy. Since the beginning, since Wister's Virginian, the cowboy has been an ideological fantasy as well as a lifestyle one. He's a vision of the ideal "American" that came straight out of the discourses of late-19th century racism that MacDougal represents.

Owen Wister himself wasn't born in the West. He was born in Philadelphia, in 1860, to an old-money family that had powerful, and complicated, roots. His grandmother was Fanny Kemble, a famous British stage actress and abolitionist; his grandfather was Pierce Butler, a rich Philadelphian and Confederate sympathizer who inherited a massive plantation complex that appalled his wife. After growing up in a family riven by ideological fault lines, the young Wister went to Harvard, traveled in elite circles, but couldn't quite decide what to do with himself. He tried a career in music, studying the works of Wagner under Franz Liszt himself. He tried business. He tried law. Nothing really felt true to who he was, and he developed one of those classic 19th-century nervous conditions: an unclassifiable malaise that would probably be diagnosed now as depression.

Everything changed when he went West. Wister took off on a train to a relative's cattle ranch in northern Wyoming, where he supposedly left the world of big-city values behind. In truth, it wasn't exactly an unconquered wilderness. It was more like the 19th-century equivalent of Dick Cheney's pheasant preserve: an established agribusiness with absentee owners that worked well as a playground for the bored and indecisive wealthy. But he became obsessed with the lifestyle there, and he spent years recording his experiences in short stories and memoirs that he sent to Eastern periodicals. As his biographer Darwin Payne put it, "He found a spiritual home, very different from Boston or Europe, which could now nourish and sustain him for many years."

The theme park in *Westworld* darkly literalizes this idea that the West is a place where one can finally discover the Self. Eastern elites pay exorbitant fees—$1,000 per day in the 1973 original film; $40,000 a day in HBO's new version—to unlock their true potential. "It doesn't cater to your lowest self," says the Man in Black, who, like Wister, is a wealthy man who becomes addicted to the park's thrills: "It reveals your deepest self. It shows you who you really are." One of the ingenious things about creator Michael Crichton's premise is that this dystopic business model has a basis in historical reality. The West really *was* Westworld for a certain class of bored aristocrat at the end of the 19th century. It really *was* framed as the place where the vigors of frontier life could cure a malaise of body and soul. Just as late-Victorian men, feeling stifled and emasculated by the luxurious trappings of London life, traveled to the colonies to reinvigorate themselves by hunting big game, getting a tan, and mingling with the natives, their American counterparts sought regeneration in a theme-park version of the open range.

So it isn't all that surprising that Wister dedicated the second edition of *The Virginian* to his old friend, Teddy

Roosevelt, whom he called "the greatest benefactor we people have known since Lincoln." Like Wister, Roosevelt had gone West in an attempt to counter the existential rot of a pampered life in the East. The extravagant murals and statues of New York's Museum of Natural History testify to his obsession with the "strenuous life," in which he felt he'd been forged into a leader of men.

Wister and Roosevelt shared another outgrowth of this obsession: a way of thinking about American history that construed their own experiences—macho contests with various forms of "savagery" on the Frontier—as both the engine of American progress and the only hope for our salvation. In the decades before he became President, Roosevelt had been a historian, and in his histories of the nation—particularly *The Winning of the West*—he had advanced his own version of Turner's "Frontier Thesis," arguing that the material hardships of frontier life had been the primary source of America's egalitarian values and democratic character. But there was one major difference. Turner's frontier heroes were the humble yeoman farmers on the frontlines of Westward expansion, scraping together a better life for themselves just as the Puritans had done before them, and just as the immigrants would do in later chapters of American history. The protagonist of American history that Roosevelt imagined was very different: a Daniel

Boone, a Davy Crockett, a solitary hunter, a frontier superhero. A "man who knows Indians" but takes their land by force. A man of "violence and conquest" who, as Richard Slotkin describes him in *Gunfighter Nation*, "lives outside the cash nexus of commercial society, in a pre-capitalist Eden [...] yet gives his life, or destroys his own 'natural' mode of living, for the sake of [a] bourgeois society whose rewards he does not value and whose manner of earning bread he despises."

Roosevelt's theory of American history had deeply racist implications. He argued not only that American progress depended on the subjugation of the natives, but also that our nation could only ever progress through the Anglo-Saxon frontier heroism of what Nietzsche would call an Übermensch. In Roosevelt's worldview, the degenerate city suppressed and feminized the Anglo-Saxon, but the frontier's Darwinian contests could bring him back to his full potential, earning him what Slotkin calls a "neo-aristocratic right to rule." This was Calvin Candie racism, phrenology-head racism, Harold MacDougal racism—but it was at the core of Roosevelt's historical writings and political appeal. It was at the core of the fantasy that the West could unlock the Self, provided that you were the right kind of Self. And it was at the core of Wister's vision of the cowboy. In an article for *Harper's Monthly* in 1895, Wister imagined what would happen if an effete British aristocrat tried his hand at ranching:

> Directly the English nobleman smelt Texas, the slumbering Saxon awoke in him, and mindful of the tournament, mindful of the hunting-field, galloped howling after wild cattle, a born horseman, a perfect athlete, and spite of the peerage and gules and argent, fundamentally kin with the drifting vagabonds who swore and galloped by his side.

In Wister's fantasy, the purpose of America is not to give freedom to the enchained, or opportunity to the oppressed. Instead, it's a proving-ground where the same old elites display their rightful mastery over everyone else. The tournament, the hunt, the horse race—all the games of the rich show up again on the Western plains. They're just real this time.

The Virginian contains a very weird passage in which the whole point of its hero becomes almost horrifyingly explicit. "Equality is a great big bluff," says the cowboy. "It's easy called." The idea is elaborated on by the narrator, a thin stand-in for Wister who develops a whole theory about what "equality" really means:

There can be no doubt of this: All America is divided into two classes, the quality and the equality. The latter will always recognize the former when mistaken for it. Both will be with us until our women bear nothing but kings. It was through the Declaration of Independence that we Americans acknowledged the eternal inequality of man. For by it we abolished a cut-and-dried aristocracy. We had seen little men artificially held up in high places, and great men artificially held down in low places, and our own justice-loving hearts abhorred this violence to human nature. Therefore, we decreed that every man should thenceforth have equal liberty to find his own level. By this very decree we acknowledged and gave freedom to true aristocracy, saying, 'Let the best man win, whoever he is.' Let the best man win! That is America's word. That is true democracy. And true democracy and true aristocracy are one and the same thing.

Sure, the Declaration of Independence states plainly that "all men are created equal." But what it really *means*, according to Wister's interpretation, is that all men should be treated equally in the eyes of the law so that they can reveal their essential *inequality* in the eyes of nature. American democracy is the one system of government in which the natural superiority of people of a certain stock can finally become self-evident, even if they're simple ranch-hands. The point of the frontier is to provide a place where this contest of racial supremacy happens. Wister's vision of the cowboy is this ideology given flesh, written into the land: The Western creates a world, as Tompkins puts it, in which the moral, physical, and social supremacy of a certain kind of white male "never appear[s] to reflect the interests or beliefs of any particular group, or of human beings at all, but seem[s] to have been dictated primordially by nature itself."

Where did this fantasy come from? Historians have discussed the Western as a reaction to late-19th century urbanization and industrialization, which seems true enough. But to Wister and Roosevelt, the problems that plagued the modern city—inequality, overcrowding, labor disputes—were all contributors to a larger existential threat: the waning power of the white man. Some Westerns make monsters out of the possibility of miscegenation or racial pollution. In others, the city is the monster, sapping the white man of his racial strength by exposing him to amoral commerce, or unnatural technology, or, more implicitly, the ways of African Americans and immigrants and Jews. Such myths are fueled by the fear that the white man will lose his grip on the world.

Red Dead rejects and mocks this viewpoint by giving it to MacDougall, a raving, cocaine-addicted, phrenology -obsessed crank. But it's still buried in the deepest source code of the Western, and even the most leftist, revisionist works in the genre have trouble shaking it off completely. No matter how much a Western degrades the cowboy, complicates him, or plunges him into the moral and physical muck, it's still hard for the genre to decenter him. It's still hard for a Western to challenge the idea that he's a vision of natural man. And it's hard to square *Red Dead*'s obvious distaste for MacDougal with a few problems that plague the game: the almost total invisibility of African-American characters; the game's studious adherence to a history of Hollywood whitewashing that ignores the historical reality of actual cowboys (who were largely Black, Mexican, Native American, and Mestizo); and the aura of inherent superiority that *Red Dead* gives Marston anyway, despite his failings, through the basic centrality of a video game protagonist. After all, what is a shooter if *not* an interactive crucible where a different kind of two-class system takes shape—where the wheat defeats the chaff, the One defeats the Many, and the man of superhuman skill conquers all? The fact that Marston, a white man, is the game's playable hero is itself a kind of aristocratic distinction. There's only one Marston: conscious, individual, powerful, free. Everyone else is just—to borrow a term weaponized by contemporary white supremacists—NPCs.

•

Yet Marston is indisputably a different breed of cowboy than the hero Wister invented. He's more ambiguous, more internally conflicted—compromised, both in the sense that he trails the heavy weight of a history of violence behind him, and in the sense that he often brokers deals between equally degenerate forces. "I'm no moralist, sir," he says. His actions—or rather, the often despicable actions the game asks you to perform *with* him—show the truth of that. He's more pragmatic than principled, always willing to play ball with people across the spectrum from conventional morality to deranged immorality. (As a character warns him during the Nuevo Paraíso chapter, "Just be careful, John. Keep jumping from one side of the fence to the other, you might just get impaled on it.") He exhibits weariness more than manliness—he's past his prime, like Gary Cooper in *Man of the West* or Clint Eastwood in *Unforgiven*. He's a committed family man, but maybe not because he's intrinsically good. Maybe because he's been doing this for a long time, and little else seems to offer any kind of solace.

Westerns often heighten the cowboy's allure by teasing his intro, making it the long, slow payoff of a train ride into another world. At the beginning of *The Virginian*, the cowboy appears outside the window of the train as it finally comes to a halt. The narrator catches a glimpse of a man of pure, coiled power, perched upon a wooden railing: a man who can rustle the most reluctant ponies, a man who "knows his business." At the beginning of *Once Upon a Time in the West*, we wait for nearly ten minutes, watching a squad of grizzled banditos slapping the flies off their beards, until the train deposits Charles Bronson on the other side of the station: silent, steely-eyed, playing a line on the harmonica that sounds a lot like *Red Dead*'s mournful jingles. In HBO's *Westworld*, park guests wait for the cowboy to appear before realizing that he's stepping off the train with them—Teddy Flood (James Marsden), the cardboard hero, with his broad hat and broader smile. The park's overseers know all too well that wanting to see him is entangled with wanting to be him.

Red Dead begins in a similar way, with a cowboy and a train ride. But its opening also does some things that are very, very different. The game's first shot shows us another new form of mass transit: a steamer pulling into port, teeming with crowds of people who look like the proverbial "huddled masses" docking at Ellis Island, ready to start their lives. As we zoom in closer, however, it becomes clear that they're not immigrants at all; they're well-off, clad in puffy dresses and Victorian finery. Among them walks a man who doesn't look like them—lean, lanky, with a wide leather hat and a dead look of purpose in his eyes. A crane hoists a motorcar from the boat to the bustling street; the crowd from the boat thins out, eager to start their business, literally leaving the man behind. The camera centers on him and reveals him to us with an epic twang. His pose is serious yet relaxed, two hands at the ready, brimming with the potential energy of a natural-born killer. Yet he isn't alone, like Bronson or the Virginian: He's in custody, flanked by federal agents in bowler hats and fancy suits. When he gets on the train, his fellow passengers—many of whom were on the boat—prattle smugly about how "civilization" has been brought to "this savage land." He still makes his journey from East to West. He still travels, by train, from the city to a different planet. But the East is here now, here already, and the West is not quite there anymore. The West is a tiny place, slowly dying in the East's shadow. The game knows that to introduce the cowboy with a train ride is to call back to the origins of the genre. It's an act of ritual, of reanimation. But the game also knows that Westerns make meaning by diverging from tradition. The game suggests Marston's difference through the train, through the cuffs, through the people who pay him no mind.

The game also suggests that he's a different breed of cowboy through the presence of a *true* cowboy from a previous generation: Landon Ricketts. Marston meets Ricketts in Chuparosa, shortly after he arrives in Nuevo Paraíso. Like the Sam Elliot dream-cowboy who speaks to The Dude in *The Big Lebowski*, Landon has a low, languorous voice, a twinkle in his eye, and an air of unreality about him. He seems to have been dropped in from another time, another version of the West less consumed by the soul-sucking standards and practices of modernity. If Marston stands in for the "Death of the West," as Rockstar's Christian Cantamessa put it, Landon is a holdover from the "Myth of the West," the John Wayne golden age. A man of principles and reserve, a man of decorum and refinement who only kills for good reasons. He immediately chastises Marston for murdering three men who tried to take his hat:

Ricketts: Oh, very good. Very good indeed, sir. What a great way to improve border relations. An illiterate farmer crossing the river, coming into this civilization and butchering the local peasants. Thank you very much, sir.

Marston: Don't mention it, old man.

Ricketts: You kill peasants, you become a peasant.

Marston: I never aspired to be anything more.

Ricketts could have easily been the protagonist of *Red Dead*, fighting for the people, fighting out of honor (although it's worth noting how much this early scene reveals a deeper racism and classism beneath his man-of-the-people sheen). But he isn't the hero of *Red Dead*; Marston is. And the game creates a contrast between them for a reason: because Marston embodies what the cowboy ended up becoming after the dream of the cowboy died.

When did the dream of the cowboy die? The early 60s is one answer. Hollywood never stopped making old-fashioned Westerns in the 60s, but they became increasingly irrelevant at the box office, and critics were quick to register how creaky and antiquated they felt in a new climate of change and political disillusionment. "Going to a Western these days for simplicity or heroism or grandeur or meaning is about like trying to mate with an ox," wrote film critic Pauline Kael in 1967, in an article blasting an artless remake of *Stagecoach* that attempted, yet again, to recapture the magic of seeing John Wayne hoist himself onto a saddle and save the day. So the genre adapted to new times, creating with it a newer, darker version of the cowboy. In the classical Westerns of the 30s, 40s, 50s—the Westerns of Eisenhower and American exceptionalism, the Westerns embodied by Landon Ricketts—the cowboy is the solution to the problems that plague the land. He's an agent of essential goodness who finally brings justice, or at least some kind of order, to a lawless place. In the revisionist Westerns of the 60s and 70s—Spaghetti Westerns, *The Wild Bunch*, *Butch Cassidy and the Sundance Kid*, *The Outlaw Josey Wales*—the cowboy is a symptom of problems far larger than himself.

The Man with No Name, Clint Eastwood's mysterious gunslinger in Sergio Leone's trilogy of mid-60s Spaghetti Westerns, is the archetypical example of this shift, and one of the figures who most obviously influenced the design of Marston. The poncho outfit you unlock after completing the game's Mexico chapter is almost exactly what Eastwood wears in *A Fistful of Dollars*; like Eastwood in the film, Marston spends most of that chapter not as a hero, nor even as a villain—older Westerns prize the clean binary of "black hats" vs. "white hats"—but as a morally ambiguous third party who steps into a factional conflict with no particular stake. Despite everything we know about his backstory and his motivations, Marston can be, like Eastwood, a bit of a cipher. He can be a little like Snake in Metal Gear Solid, a game series deeply indebted to the Spaghetti Western: an anarchic operative who performs brutal acts of violence with technocratic efficiency and little more than a blank, bearded grimace.

Movies like the Eastwood Spaghetti Westerns reduce the cowboy to a kind of amoral gamesmanship. He shoots because he's good at shooting. He rides into a gang stronghold because gang strongholds are where he thrives. He cuts the noose holding his cornered nemesis—as Eastwood does at the end of *The Good, the Bad, and the Ugly*—because, like Batman and the Joker, he needs the duel to feel alive. In *High Plains Drifter*, which Eastwood also directed, he plays a mysterious stranger who shows up one day in the troubled mining town of Lago. Lago is a grim, beleaguered place living in the shadow of a kind of prophecy: In just a few days, three convicts will be released, and they will come riding into town demanding back pay from the mining company and destroying anything they can get their hands on. After seeing how he handles a gun, the town appoints the stranger as their guardian. But although he eventually defeats the bandits, he does not end up being the protector of the people. Instead, he becomes their jailer and their tormenter. The town, as it turns out, is burdened with sin. Every man and woman in it looked upon the face of a suffering fellow-citizen as he was bullwhipped to death in the middle of the street for snitching on the mining company's corruption. It's unclear how the stranger knew this man, or knew this crime, but he punishes the town for what they've done under the guise of being their protector from external threats. He makes them paint every building blood-red and writes "HELL" on the town's sign. He allows it to *become* hell when the bandits finally emerge, letting it be consumed by fire.

Marston's a little like that. He isn't really a force of good who cleanses the land of evil; instead, he inflicts sin upon the sinners, ruin upon the ruined, death upon the dead. He isn't necessarily evil, but he's part of evil's infrastructure, compounding—rather than eliminating—the suffering of the places he visits. And the game implies pretty strongly that on some level he prefers the constant, agonistic struggles of frontier gunmanship to the quiet boredom of family life. Or at least he can't live without those struggles, which aligns him with perhaps the most complex and morally ambiguous cowboy hero of all time: John Wayne in *The Searchers*.

Directed by John Ford and released in 1956, at the zenith of Wayne's popularity, *The Searchers* is a classic Western that can easily be read as a racist fantasia in tune with the original ideology of Wister and Roosevelt. Wayne plays Ethan Edwards, a proud Civil War veteran who spends years hunting the Comanches who set fire to his family's homestead and abducted his eight-year-old niece, Debbie. The racism that gave birth to the cowboy becomes the racism *of* the cowboy: He sees everything not only through the lens of a stark binary of good vs.

evil, but also through the lens of a grand racial contest in which the white race is losing ground. He views the Comanches as inhuman, and mixing with them as a way of becoming less human yourself. "Fella could mistake you for a half-breed," he says, upon returning home and seeing the complexion of his nephew Martin Pawley. Martin is "an eighth Cherokee"—enough for Ethan to deny the fact that they're related by blood.

At times it can be hard to say whether the movie endorses Ethan's racism or critiques it. It doesn't exactly represent the Comanches sympathetically, even if, as we learn later, their war chief Scar set fire to the homestead out of revenge for his murdered sons. Still, the movie distances itself from Ethan *through* Martin, through the contrast between old and new. Martin is the new generation: young, impassioned, hot-headed, reckless. Ethan is the old: cool, cynical, tactical, taciturn. But he's also slouching toward obsolescence, even a kind of monstrosity. When they finally find Debbie at a Comanche camp, she has become Scar's war bride. Ethan's first instinct is not to save her, nor even to talk to her, but to shoot her in cold blood.

Martin looks up to Ethan, but his psychological journey over the course of the film—and maybe Ethan's, too—involves coming to recognize just how much the cowboy lifestyle has rendered Ethan incapable of feeling. At one point, Ethan tells Martin that he's leaving all his goods and worldly possessions to him. It's a scene that, in any other Western, would be played for melodrama: The fatherless boy adopted by a noble father figure. But Martin resists. He knows that to completely surrender himself to Ethan's lifestyle is to abandon things that still matter to him—the fiancée waiting at home; the hearth and its creature comforts; a whole universe of goodness from which the cowboy cuts himself off. The film creates many sharp contrasts between a world of over-the-top Victorian domesticity, centered on the family, and the outer world that Ethan inhabits—a world that is for men, by men, and focused only on manly things. It begins and ends, famously, with shots of the house's threshold—the portal that divides these two realms, just as it divides light and darkness, innocence and brutality. Ethan comes in through the threshold, awkwardly, at the beginning of the film. At the end he remains outside, as if he knows that the life he's led, this life of cowboy heroism, has finally left him unable to reintegrate himself into a society that is moving on. He will always be an outsider. The largest threat in the film is not the Comanches but the possibility that Martin will become an eternal outsider, too.

There's a mission toward the end of *Red Dead* called "John Marston and Son." It's one of the series of mundane and ominously quiet tasks that the game asks you to perform once Marston returns to his ranch and his family. The mission begins with Marston telling Jack, his son, to get his head out of Western adventure novels and come learn how to track elk. He explains that the myths of the West are dead, and tries instead to teach Jack how to live in a time of realism and hardscrabble practicality. As Marston, you kill the elk with the same perfect, brutal efficiency as always; it's like any other kill in the game. But Jack is the one who gets on his knees to skin the beast, and there's something horrible about the grimace he makes to the camera—the unnatural way that he grits his teeth through one of the game's most mundane and ordinary tasks. In the next mission, John and Abigail muse about how their son might end up having a different life:

> Abigail: I look at Jack… I look at him and feel blessed. Maybe he can become something more.
>
> John: He can be whatever he wants to be. He ain't gonna be no frontier gunslinger, killing and running in no gang though. That way's over. Railroads and motor cars and government gone and done away with all that.

And yet Jack does become John; when John dies, the game cuts to a man standing at his grave with the same gear, the same grimace. The son can pick up exactly where his father left off. Marston's right: In this new world, Jack is doomed to be even more of an anachronism. But that doesn't prevent him from becoming the walking dead.

•

What is the cowboy? Is he a force of good or a force of corruption, staining everything he touches? Do we want to be him, or do we fear becoming him? Does he stand against the poisonous effects of his environment, or is he just another manifestation of the cold, Darwinian logic of an unforgiving place? *Red Dead*, like *The Searchers*, asks these questions. In doing so, it aligns itself with an era in the history of the genre when the Western transformed irrevocably from a form of art based on moral certainties into a form of art in which there were none. And when the cowboy himself transformed from Wister's dubious ideal into an agent of amoral chaos.

This is what George Lucas was talking about when he said, in August 1977, that he had been inspired to make *Star Wars* after he "saw the Western die." In box office terms, yes, fewer Westerns than ever were being made in the late 70s, leaving the field of cultural production wide open for new genres (the gangster epic, the superhero blockbuster, Star Wars itself) to become the vehicles of American self-mythology. But you only need to glance at the Star Wars mythos—Jedi vs. Sith in a dualistic, crypto-religious struggle between darkness and light; a desert of deprivation that refines the pure heroism of the protagonist; a struggle between freedom and all-consuming order—to understand what he really meant. The Western had long ceased to be morally pure. It had descended into depravity and anarchy. Generations of nerds have decried Lucas's decision to edit the cantina scene in the 1997 Special Edition of *Star Wars* so that Greedo, rather than Han Solo, shoots first. Han shot Greedo first because he was originally modeled off of Sergio Leone's deceitful Western antiheroes. Lucas made Greedo shoot Han because, as he later explained to the *Washington Post*:

> I was thinking mythologically—should he be a cowboy, should he be John Wayne? And I said, "Yeah, he should be John Wayne." And when you're John Wayne, you don't shoot people [first]—you let them have the first shot. It's a mythological reality that we hope our society pays attention to.

In other words, he created *Star Wars*—at least partly—as an attempt to reclaim what the Western had been before: a "mythological" narrative centered on a certain kind of hero. Lucas hadn't just seen the Western die; he'd seen the cowboy die. *Star Wars* was an attempt to revive the cowboy after he had decayed into something dark and wholly different. (It's ironic that the Western *Star Wars* tries to reanimate the most, sometimes shot-for-shot, is *The Searchers*—the film with the most complex and morally dubious version of the John Wayne hero.)

No matter how compromised it makes Marston, no matter how morally dubious, *Red Dead*, too, wants to revive that mythic hero. I see a lot of the Virginian in him, left over from the birth of the genre: the air of decency, the dry wit, the ease in an uneasy place. The appearance of natural superiority, revealed through Darwinian struggle. It's hard to imagine playing as him otherwise—playing as a figure like Eastwood's stranger in *High Plains Drifter*, sadistic and nearly silent, with no moral code or sense of decency pushing him into war against the enemy. After all, one of the appeals of playing *Red Dead Redemption* in the first place is the prospect of playing as a different kind of protagonist— an old-fashioned hero, not yet exposed to the morally corrosive effects of modernity. Rockstar makes it easy to mock people like Jimmy Saint, the effete Easterner obsessed with Marston's frontier virility, not entirely recognizing that they—and we—are a little bit like him.

But I also see the psychodrama of Ethan Edwards playing out beneath Marston's furrowed brow. The idea that being a cowboy is itself corrosive to the body and the soul; the idea that, once you give yourself over to that life, you can never become yourself again. You can never go home. To look at *Red Dead* next to the history of the Western—against the backdrop of the genre's gradual transformation from racist, masculinist dreams into disenchanted nightmares—is to realize that "Red Dead Redemption" is a deeply fitting title, because redemption might be the central question of the cowboy. Is the cowboy our redeemer or our tormenter—our savior or the symbol of our inability to be saved? Can he ever be redeemed himself?

It depends on what you see when the train slows down, the desert stands still, and you finally get a good look at the man outside.

VIOLENCE

WHEN I PLAY *RED DEAD* NOW, I think about a visit with my dad. It was in the period of time after my mom had divorced him and not long before he died, when he'd remade his apartment into a kind of museum of Margini history—old black and white photos of Italians all over the wall, like the back of a pizzeria—and when his voluble discourses were increasingly uncensored and unfiltered. I came over, sat on the old flowery couch that my mom had left behind, and he talked to me about politics, God, his old in-laws, his past wives. He kept playing with the automatic armchair, moving it up and down as he talked, and his large, bald head seemed to float before me like the spirit of a great and mischievous sage. Then, all of a sudden, as the monologue was dying down, he asked me: "You want a gun?"

With a little skip in his step, he lumbered over to an old shoebox and took it out: a sleek six-bullet revolver with a wooden grip, unusable—it no longer had a firing pin—but otherwise in pristine condition. It was clearly old, probably late-19th century, but it had the heft and feel of a modern, reliable product—a simple mechanism refined over generations of killing. I found myself compulsively spinning the chamber, feeling the click, trying to imagine who had owned it, what they'd done with it, whether it had been involved in any wars or violent misdeeds. He didn't give me any straight answers about its provenance, only that he'd found it during his "archeological" surveys of the apartment's most buried and inaccessible crap. In my house now, I keep it in a box full of other objects he gave me: a pair of Italian Navy binoculars used by my grandfather during World War II; a scale model of a human skull; a piece of fake plastic feces he always referred to, impishly, as "the shit." Together they would make a pretty strange Vermeerian still life.

I think about that gun when I watch Marston reload his revolver—my revolver—with impossible speed and fluency. As a genre, the Western contains multitudes, an incalculable variety of stories within the same mythic space. But a Western wouldn't be a Western without guns. The image of a man with a gun constitutes the moral and aesthetic center of almost any Western film. Depending on the film's point of view, he stands in for a history of violence either sacred or profane.

In his essay on Westerns, Robert Warshow makes a meaningful distinction between cowboys and gangsters.

The gangster commits violence wantonly; the cowboy, only when necessary. When the gangster commits violence, he does so for himself. When the cowboy commits violence, he does so in the name of an ideal—maybe justice, but more likely honor, a neo-medieval value system that doesn't always reflect what is legal but always corresponds to what is right. This *restrained* violence is what gives the cowboy his aura of moral purity:

> The Westerner could not fulfill himself if the moment did not finally come when he can shoot his enemy down. But because that moment is so thoroughly the expression of his being, it must be kept pure. He will not violate the accepted forms of combat though by doing so he could save a city. And he can wait.

The cowboy's violence is crisp, economical, necessary. It doesn't need to happen now, but it will happen at "an appointed time" (to quote the title of one of *Red Dead*'s missions), and it will bring order back to the land. The quick and decisive release of his power will put an end to the kind of violence that he stands against: the gratuitous, dishonorable slaughter committed by less principled forces.

That, at least, might have been generally true in the era of the "classical" Western. But just as the Westerns of the 60s and 70s changed the nature of the cowboy dramatically, letting him slump from his pedestal into the moral murk of his enemies, they also depleted gun violence of all its moral certainties. You see fewer and fewer duels at high noon in the Westerns of the Vietnam era, fewer and fewer symmetrical conflicts between the forces of good and evil. The gunfight gave way to the "gundown": the messy and indiscriminate slaughter of both enemies and civilians.

Red Dead taps into this era in the history of the Western's violence. A man with a gun leers from the game's box art—Marston at his most disheveled, grimacing, hair parted by dirt and sweat. Unlike other box-art heroes, who might be resting a gun on their broad shoulders (*Bioshock Infinite*) or reloading it under fire, he points a sawed-off shotgun right at us, as if we were the cowering foe—on our knees, looking up at him—who might bring his revenge cycle to a close. But we won't. No one will. His gaze invites us into a world where violence is never clean.

Yet it also invites us into a world where violence means something—and where different acts of violence can mean very different things. More than almost any other shooter I can think of, *Red Dead* loads its violence with cultural, historical, and moral baggage, asking the player to think about their involvement, even their complicity, in systems that sprawl beyond the bullet that goes into the brain. It might seem at first like one of those games that raises all its questions and themes in cutscenes, leaving the "gameplay" part divorced from the larger project of making the player feel and think. But the forms of violence it asks you to commit—especially those it asks you to commit routinely—are deeply evocative in themselves.

Dead Eye

The game's "Dead Eye" system is one of the few things it retains from *Red Dead Revolver*, and also one of the few things that allows Marston to become a bona fide superhero. Click the right analog stick on the controller and a blanket of orange slo-mo will envelop the scene, allowing him to plan as many shots as there are bullets in his gun; release the stick and he will execute, pumping the bullets into his targets with robotic speed and efficiency. The move calls to mind several cinematic touchstones: modern blockbusters like *The Matrix* and *300*, where slo-mo creates stylish scenes of balletic violence and grimacing beards; that scene in the first *Iron Man* where Tony Stark uses an advanced multi-targeting system to automagically distinguish civilians from terrorists; Spaghetti Westerns like *A Fistful of Dollars* and *The Good, the Bad, and the Ugly*, where Clint Eastwood pulls the trigger and, in half a second, five men drop to the ground. But the game has another association in mind when you look at what's happening during Dead Eye and see the devastation it wreaks: the movies of Sam Peckinpah. Peckinpah was the first to bring slo-mo to the Western, and he used it to reveal not the skill of the gunfighter but the deaths of his victims. Limbs shattering. The knees of horses buckling. Clouds of blood pillowing out of muddy clothes. This is what you see in Peckinpah. And it's what you see in Dead Eye.

Often cited as a key influence on *Red Dead* and its sequel, Peckinpah's 1969 film *The Wild Bunch* might be the closest thing to the game's style, sensibility, and soul. The film takes place in the same historical period as *Red Dead*, in a similar kind of setting: a region on the border between the U.S. and Mexico, circa 1913. Technology is advancing. The frontier has been closed for decades. The West is about to die. The railroad company, even more than the federal government, has colonized the land, generating the film's very *Red Dead*-like plot: After capturing an aging outlaw named Deke Thornton, the company forces him to hunt down the other members of his former gang.

Red Dead 1 and *2* focus on different halves of this story. *Red Dead 2* centers on the gang—the charismatic renegades quixotically seeking freedom in a land where freedom is no longer possible. *Red Dead 1* centers on the gang's pursuer, a role which doesn't get as much screen time in *The Wild Bunch* and comes to seem more than a little pathetic in comparison to its antiheroes. The movie not only sidelines Deke narratively, but also saddles him with incompetent mercenaries who keep bumbling the operation; his plot is played for laughs. But that comedy feeds into a tragedy that is arguably much more tragic than the story of the outlaws. They get to be martyrs for their own deluded dream; he can only be a scavenger, a rat, sniffing around the detritus they've left behind. Following the trail of the Wild Bunch, Deke berates his useless mercenaries, revealing an obsession with his old gang that takes us all the way back to the alluring virility of Wister's cowboy:

> They know what this is all about! And what do I have? Nothing but you egg-sucking, chicken-stealing gutter trash, with not even 60 rounds between you. We're after men. And I wish to God I was with them.

Deke wishes he could join up with the Bunch one last time. Marston is never quite so envious of the men he hunts, but at certain points throughout the game— when the federal agents controlling him sneer with condescension, breathe down his neck—you almost wish that he could do the same.

Of course, that wouldn't necessarily mean joining something good or pure. Violence is never pure in *The Wild Bunch*, no matter who's committing it. Nor is it ever necessary. The film, like the game, racks up an astronomical body count, presenting civilian casualties as a routine byproduct of the gunfighter lifestyle. At the beginning of the film, in what's supposed to be their last heist, the gang attempts to rob the railroad offices where a cache of silver is being stored. There's only one problem: Deke has caught up to them. The two sides start firing at each other in open daylight, as a Temperance Union parade marches through the crowded Main Street. In slow motion, we watch as church-going anti-booze crusaders tumble forward into the dust with bullets in their backs. It feels like a sequence from *Saving Private Ryan*. Another kind of Western wouldn't show us so many casualties among the innocent and the undeserving, but *The Wild Bunch* aims to sully the clean symmetries of the classic shootout with something like the messiness of war.

The Wild Bunch came out a year after US troops slaughtered scores of Vietnamese civilians in the My Lai Massacre, and it's hard not to see an image of that massacre in the gundown that opens the film. The film's gratuitous aesthetic carried political stakes: It wanted to destroy the well of metaphors—images of crisp, justified, necessary Western violence—that politicians and other hawkish public figures had drawn from in their defenses of the war. The first and foremost was John Wayne himself, who made use of his own status as an icon of American heroism in pro-war rallies as well as the jingoistic, pro-Vietnam war film *The Green Berets*. (To this day, *Time* magazine special editions lining the checkout aisles at suburban supermarkets celebrate Wayne as though he were a Vietnam hero, even though he never served.) President Lyndon B. Johnson also facilitated an imaginative link between the Western and the war when, during a trip to Cam Ranh Bay in 1967, he delivered a pep talk urging the Army to "nail that coonskin to the wall." As J. Hoberman points out in his essay "How the Western was Lost," pro-war rhetoric in the Vietnam era was full of deliberate efforts to turn Indochina into "an extension of the Western frontier"—and to turn Americans, once again, into "settlers, cavalrymen, schoolmarms, gunslingers, and marshals on a mission of protection and progress." *The Wild Bunch* set out to undermine these metaphors by making the West itself a place of massacres and moral decay. In the film, no one is "on a mission of protection and progress." There are only outlaws and former outlaws gunning each other down in spectacles of apocalyptic violence.

The film creates an atmosphere of political and moral nihilism that feeds directly into *Red Dead*'s sensibility, just as similarly nihilistic 70s gangster flicks like Scorsese's *Mean Streets* lurk in the background of other Rockstar games. After the massacre at the beginning of *The Wild Bunch*, enterprising spectators come and inspect the bodies for cash, bullets, and everyday supplies. The same thing can happen if Marston guns down the good people of Armadillo: People will come waddling over, unfazed. You can see pretty much every element of the Rockstar aesthetic—cool-kid cynicism, political nihilism, casual misogyny, violence that functions as a kind of punchline—in a scene that happens about midway through the film. After fleeing from the botched heist, Pike's gang ends up in Mexico, at the compound of a cartoonishly depraved generalissimo. One member of the gang, Angel, sees that the generalissimo has stolen his girlfriend. He responds by shooting her. But even more demented than his response is the response of the Generalissimo and the entire compound: a chorus of cackling, maniacal laughter as she bleeds out on the pavement.

Gatling Gun

In another move that anticipates *Red Dead*, *The Wild Bunch* weds its slow-motion aesthetic to a kind of violence that is in no way slow-motion: the carnage created by machine guns. It is sometimes pointed out that Dr. Richard J. Gatling invented the Gatling gun for the purpose of reducing wartime casualties: "It occurred to me," he said, "that if I could invent a machine—a gun—which could by its rapidity of fire, enable one man to do as much battle duty as a hundred, that it would, to a large extent supersede the necessity of large armies, and consequently, exposure to battle and disease [would] be greatly diminished." *The Wild Bunch* makes a mockery of Gatling's earnest optimism, presenting the gun (and its successors) as merely a tool that allows psychotic murderers to realize their most depraved fantasies. After the scene at the compound, the generalissimo pays Pike's gang to steal a machine gun from a US Army convoy. When they bring it to him after bloodshed, explosions, and incalculable collateral damage, he reacts like a kid on Christmas morning and sets it off by accident, shredding his own camp with a hail of bullets in every direction. When the dust settles, he laughs. The gang laughs; the entire camp laughs—they all cackle maniacally at the power he wields now, the ability to destroy human life as quickly as fire eats through tissue paper.

This weird, cynical, degenerate scene resonates acutely with some of the machine gun sequences in *Red Dead*. In one Mexico mission, you steal a machine gun from a government train and use it to mow down soldiers. In another, you're *on* a government train and you use it to mow down rebels. In the climactic mission of the game's first chapter, an assault on Fort Mercer, you sneak into the compound, Trojan Horse-style, in the back of Nigel West Dickens's carriage full of quackery. Soon enough, you pop up to deliver apocalyptic destruction to Bill Williamson and his flunkies: As Marston cranks the machine, you guide the target reticle from one little speck of a man to another, smushing them like ants under the unstoppable hail of bullets. The mounted gun is an ancient shooter trope, a fixture of *Halo* and every other game you can think of, but this one feels more consequential than most. *Red Dead* isn't the kind of game—or the kind of world—where automatic weapons at this scale have become everyday tools of the trade. The relative austerity of the game's action turns the Gatling gun sequences into overwhelming spectacles.

But maybe not as overwhelming as they should be, given the Gatling gun's power. Even if it's loud, and even if the carnage is over-the-top, using the Gatling gun in *Red Dead* still feels a little like doing a scratch-off, or carefully popping all the bubbles in a sheet of bubble-wrap. There's a feeling of *control*—of deliberate, meticulous precision—that undermines the atmosphere of chaos that *Red Dead* borrows from Peckinpah. There's a difference in affect, too: In *The Wild Bunch*, the Gatling gun elicits terror (on the part of its victims) and glee (on the part of its user). In *Red Dead*, it elicits businesslike disaffection. Marston operates the hot, hellish machine with the cold efficiency of a machine himself—an efficiency the game almost mocks in a late mission that finds him using one at the behest of his government handlers. Marston mans a Gatling gun in the back of a truck driven through the streets of town by the cackling federal agents, who understand just how much power they have and what the thing can do. He ends up killing a lot of people with that gun: mainly outlaws and Native Americans in the employ of Dutch van der Linde, his former leader and quasi-father. But before he does, the agents drive him past crowds of people who look upon the contraption in awe and horror, saying things like "My oh my, that's the devil's work!" Marston remains uncharacteristically silent, unusually passive. He's in the backseat of an ugly death machine, chugging forward with grim inexorability—the kind of machine that will claim countless lives in four short years, in the trenches of World War I. In his essay "The Storyteller," critic and philosopher Walter Benjamin imagines a figure called the Angel of History who looks backward, in horror, at all the atrocities of the 20th century. Marston is kind of like that in this sequence, but he's looking forward: to the trenches, the camps, the bomb, the towers—all the horrors that technological advances will bring. Yet his utter steeliness, his completely robotic servitude, might be even more alarming than the atrocities he portends. Marston is placid; he himself is an omen of the technological violence yet to come.

In the classical Western, violence is served at a human scale, one-to-one. Violence matters. Every shot rings into the empty desert like a decisive, resounding thunderclap. In *Red Dead*, violence has become routinized. Dead Eye is the ability that makes Marston superhuman—the fastest gun in the West. It's also one of the things that makes him inhuman, together with the endless surge of the machine gun and the way he can dispatch foes one after another with quick, lever-like pulls of the left and right triggers.

If the rhythm of his killing feels machinelike, it may be due to the nature of the medium: Video games are human-machine interfaces that sometimes struggle to eliminate the cold sensibility of the machine. What you do in video games can inevitably feel like performing subroutines, as though you've yoked yourself, cyborg-like, to the brain of a being that thinks in binary. Then again, in his memoir *Gamelife*, Michael W. Clune insists that this is exactly what makes video games particularly effective as a medium—the way they can use repetition to dig into the player's psyche:

Everything that happens in a computer game happens ten thousand times. Because computer games mimic habit, they get through to us. They teach us about the big things in a way nothing else can. They teach us about death, about character, about fate, about action and identity. They turn insights into habits. The habits bore through our defenses. Computer games reach us.

In *Red Dead*, you use Marston's gun to lock onto a man and shoot him in the face, or the arm, or the belly, ten thousand times. You turn on the slow-motion targeting system like Iron Man and shoot five, six, eight men at once—ten thousand times. What does all this repetition teach us? Does it teach us anything? Maybe only the idea that violence can become like Dead Eye: a subroutine of the self.

Hunting

Before it introduces any of its human characters, *The Wild Bunch* begins with a disturbing image of nature: three white scorpions being devoured by a teeming pile of fire ants. The scorpions look deadly, but they thrash and thrash hopelessly while the ants suck them into an inescapable red morass. We watch this for a few seconds; then the camera shows us who else is watching: a gang of kids, bedraggled and silent, viewing the spectacle with sadistic smiles and glassy eyes. The contest between scorpions and ants introduces us to the world of the film, where amoral violence is the norm. It's a Darwinian world where violence is the law of things; nothing is going to apologize. But the fact that kids are watching this spectacle—the fact that the kids have *made* these creatures duke it out in a kind of mini-Thunderdome, for their own entertainment— introduces us to something darker: the way humans use nature to authorize their own cruelty.

Like the Western, open world games depend on animals. They want us to see how many creeping things creepeth in the background, how many birds fly over-head, how many species can be collected in the bestiary by amateur gamer zoologists. Their purpose is clear enough: Nothing makes a digital space seem *alive* like the feeling that there's an ecosystem around the player, composed by AI-driven critters with their own patterns of behavior. Hyrule in *Ocarina of Time* would be a much more abstract realm without its chickens, its fish, and especially its bugs—the bugs that scurry into little holes in the ground when Link picks up a rock. The jungles of *Metal Gear Solid 3* would feel sterile and predictable without green tree pythons and cobalt blue tarantulas stalking the foliage under Snake's feet. In a similar way, the rural world of *Red Dead* wouldn't feel nearly as real without beavers and rabbits scampering around, crows swarming over Marston's corn silo, horses that buck the rider, and cows that stray from the herd. The animals send a message: This is a living place, and therefore a real one. It doesn't need you. It may even go on without you. The creatures will do their own thing, and you can continue doing yours.

In truth, though, you don't always leave them alone. You also kill them, en masse, and sell their pelts and horns and organs to buy new guns and bullets and outfits. If *Red Dead* was the first open world game to present a realistic ecosystem, it was also the first open world game to present antagonistic interactions with nature as one of its bedrock appeals. It popularized another design element simultaneously: the hunting-skinning gameplay loop, in which the open-world protagonist fights animals—especially carnivorous predators—and collects raw materials from their carcasses.

You see a coyote, a wolf, a wild boar, or a noble buck. Maybe it's attacking you. Or maybe you've caught it unawares, after dropping bait and hiding behind a rock like the skilled man of the woods that the game some-times, halfheartedly, asks you to be. In either case, the process is simple. You target the critter, pull the trigger, and hope for the best—or activate Dead Eye and pump it with an obscene number of bullets. What happens next has become, at this point, a ubiquitous trope of the genre: Marston bends down, plunges his knife into the creature's limp frame, and carves horizontally like he's slicing open a hero roll. Blood spatters on the camera. He stands up and receives his spoils, which now reside in the abstract realm of the menu system: 2x wolf teeth; buffalo hide; eagle feather. In *Far Cry 3* and *4*, the slash is immediately followed by the extraction of a nondescript lump of flesh; in *Assassin's Creed 3* and *4*, it's followed by a tasteful fade to black. In each game, the animal, once harvested, eventually disappears.

Red Dead 2 tries to make the process vastly more complicated. Pelts can be "poor" or "perfect" depending on the cleanliness of the kill. You can track animals by scent, scare them easily, "study" them for extensive information about their behaviors. When you finally kill them, the skinning animation is almost grotesquely detailed and specific to their anatomy: If he skins an alligator in the Lemoyne bayou, protagonist Arthur Morgan will flip the skin inside out like he's changing a duvet cover. Carcasses literally decompose as the in-game days go by. And yet, for all its attempts to be ludicrously, laboriously realistic, for all its attempts to encase the player in a display at the American Museum of Natural History, *Red Dead 2*'s predator fights are a lot like those in *Red Dead 1*. In both games, the animal encounters that truly matter are the contests with animals that can kill you. *Red Dead 1* has coyotes and wolves that roam in packs, grizzly bears in the wilds of

Tall Trees, and cougars that roam Hennigan's Stead, nearly promising insta-death to hapless Marstons that wander off the beaten path. *Red Dead 2* has "legendary animals," bigger versions of the same beasts that the game hypes like boss fights.

The Western was born in a period when writers, artists, and intellectuals were obsessed with animal power. Wister's *The Virginian* was published in 1902: one year before Jack London's *The Call of the Wild*, less than a decade before Edgar Rice Burroughs's *Tarzan of the Apes* and only a couple of decades before Ernest Hemingway would wax on and on about the beauty of bullfighting. It was published a year before Thomas Edison's production studio would demonstrate the power of film technology not only by creating the first movie Western, *The Great Train Robbery*, but also by electrocuting an elephant named Topsy on camera. So many late-Victorians wanted to dominate animals, destroy them, and possess their strength. In part, their obsession grew out of the same complex about white masculinity that gave birth to Wister's cowboy hero. Masculine anxiety fueled the outdoorsy image of Teddy Roosevelt as a hunter and frontier hero. It fueled the conservation movement, which emerged from gentlemen's hunting societies like the Boone and Crockett Club and insisted that America preserve wild spaces where noble creatures could remain free—so that intrepid Man could fight them. It even fueled the growth of Roosevelt's baby, the American Museum of Natural History, which, under the directorship of the ultra-macho Henry Fairfield Osborn, literally mounted dinosaur fossils to look like they were attacking each other in a bid to curb "effeminacy" in young boys. And of course, it fueled the Man vs. Nature spectacles in the Western: a new genre in which the white man shows dominance over the world not just through battles with Indians, but through primordial contests with beasts.

I find it hard not to view *Red Dead* as a latter-day outgrowth of this mentality, even though the game makes hunting animals secondary to hunting humans, even though Marston can get mangled by the creatures that stalk the plains, and even though, like *Red Dead* 2, it tries to emphasize survivalism by reframing in-game hunting as a matter of basic necessity rather than arcade-y spectacle. In *Educated*, Tara Westover's memoir about growing up in a family of Mormon survivalists in the Idaho mountains, she describes the painful, punishing labor of breaking feral horses:

> My brothers and I would spend days, even weeks, earning the horse's trust, just so we could touch it. Then we would stroke its long face and gradually, over more weeks, work our hands around its wide neck and down

its muscular body. After a month of this we'd bring out the saddle, and the horse would toss its head suddenly and with such violence that the halter would snap or the rope break.

The horses, Westover continues, "were pitiless, powerful avatars from another world." In *Red Dead* they're commodities. It takes Marston about ten seconds to tame one utterly, through a minigame that asks you to wiggle the control stick in the right direction. Sure, *Red Dead* isn't like the Far Cry games, where you get into some sort of epic predator fight every ten seconds, where skinning is necessary to the weapon upgrade process, and where Tarantinoesque caricatures literally tell you that you're absorbing power and testosterone from the corpses of great beasts. But it's adjacent to these fantasies of frictionless domination.

Once again, though, the late 19th century seems to be an instructive era, maybe because it's sort of a doppelganger of our own time. To say that the predator fantasies of that era were all about manhood is to miss the fact that they were also about humanness: the vulnerability of the human as a species and the fragility of the human as a category. On the one hand, the post-Darwinians felt the fear that we might *be* animals—which means we have to show our dominance over them. On the other hand, they felt the fear that we're not animal enough: that we've strayed from our bestial nature, our deepest source of power, by becoming too civilized and removing other creatures from our daily lives.

That latter fear still haunts us. As John Berger argued in his 1980 essay "Why Look at Animals?", post-industrial capitalism has left us with a yearning for contact with other creatures. Berger imagines a primeval hunter-gatherer world in which we lived with animals, learned from them, exchanged meaningful eye contact across "a narrow abyss of noncomprehension." In today's world, wild animals have been expunged from urban spaces; if we encounter them, it's a remarked-upon accident—a coyote in Brooklyn is a news story—or a problem to solve. If we desire to encounter them, all we have are zoos, cartoons, nature documentaries, and now video games—alienated spectacles that *show* us animals but also remind us of their absence.

Red Dead seems designed, like the Far Cry games, to fill this void in an ersatz way, yet it also involves the player in the very processes that produced that void in the first place. Berger pinpoints the nineteenth century as the historical moment when we finally severed ourselves from other creatures—when, through processes of industrialization and urban expansion, "every tradition which has previously mediated between man and nature was broken." You can see that *happening* in *Red Dead*; you can even take part in it. Yes, a cougar can run out from the bushes and maul you, but killing great predators isn't really a challenge. All you need to do is turn on Dead Eye, queue up a barrage of headshots, and the animal will collapse into a pathetic heap. One mission forces Marston to confront an enormous grizzly bear in the frigid wilds of Tall Trees. Unlike other bears in the game, this bear stands up on its mighty haunches and roars. In a strange kind of glitch, it will keep standing there and roaring forever if you don't do anything. The game expects you to shoot it. And you will shoot it, of course, and it will go down easily: another great icon of savage nobility, another great test of Man's strength and endurance, dispatched without ceremony or effort.

The game contains many little hunting challenges, and doles out rewards for selling as many animal parts as possible. Hunting bears in Tall Trees can be a semi-lucrative pastime. Yet *Red Dead*, unlike *Far Cry*, is lackadaisical at best about the *meaning* of these activities. They do not contribute to the crafting of permanent item upgrades, nor do they contribute to the progress of Marston himself. They only give you money—money that you can earn in other ways or ignore altogether without affecting the plot or gameplay. The game, unlike its sequel, never seems all that interested in allowing you to think that the hunting you're doing is channeling nature's strength, or communing with the land, or even doing what's necessary to survive in a harsh and bitter environment. Or even that hunting is *hard*. What it invites you to do instead is to view Marston's activities as a form of exploitation in tune with the destructive advance of modernity—a way of contributing to the extinctions and expulsions that Berger talks about.

That might be, in the end, what makes the "Manifest Destiny" achievement—which, again, you get for exterminating all twenty of the game's lumbering bison—an even darker joke than it seems. The achievement refers to a historical campaign, encouraged by the US government and aided by the US Army, to hunt bison to extinction in the mid- to late-19th century, largely as a way of forcing out the Plains Indians by depriving them of their primary food source. In 1874, General Phil Sheridan of the US Army proclaimed that buffalo hunters had "done more in the last two years, and will do more in the next year, to settle the vexed Indian question than the entire regular army has done in the last thirty years." The hunting campaign was an attempt not only to exterminate two populations in one, but to replace a whole way of life, predicated on coexistence, with a way of life predicated on consumption, colonization, and rapacious plunder. *Red Dead 2* meditates on these implications more directly in a mission where you help Charles Smith, another member of Dutch's gang, hunt down government-sponsored poachers who have left bison carcasses rotting under the sun.

The achievement also evokes *Butcher's Crossing*, a novel by John Williams (not *that* John Williams) that focuses on a bison hunt in 1870s Kansas. The novel's protagonist, Will Andrews, is a transplant from Boston who comes to the West seeking Nature with a capital N—the sublime virginity of the landscape, celebrated by what characters in *Red Dead* call "those nature writers from back East." He joins a hunt led by a man named Miller, a capitalist with intense, Daniel Plainview-like charisma. As the hunt proceeds, Andrews realizes that it bears more than a passing resemblance to the world of industrial production he has left behind. Miller shoots the bull and the others do not run. They do not fight back, charge at him, or test his mettle: Instead they stand in place, waiting to be culled with systematic precision, shot after shot, like so many of the animals that you can reduce to pulp in *Red Dead*—like the great bear that just stands there, waiting for you, begging for you, performing its choreographed pantomime of ferocity for an audience of one. You can't escape into the landscape from the great churning machine of commerce and exploitation. You can only bring the machine with you. You can only be a part of it.

●

Red Dead does many things with violence. It makes you feel good; it makes you feel dirty. It makes killing hard, or at least harder to stomach than it is in other shooters; it makes killing easy, in keeping with a world where industrialism is making all the sins of humanity easier to mass-produce. It takes the crisp action figures of the older Westerns—black hat vs. white hat, in a duel at high noon—and melts them into gooey, sticky tar that gets all over your shoes. But the game's more powerful and enigmatic effect is simply the way it makes you ask yourself: What are you doing? What are you working toward, as you move from cover to cover and ping yet another bandit with a bullet to the head? What are you becoming, as you merge with the machine?

REVOLUTION

IN THE EARLY 2000S, a Dutch maintenance man named Jos van Bedoff made a discovery that would revolutionize the design of airport bathrooms: Men are more likely to aim their piss if a little picture of a fly is painted on the urinal. I thought a lot about this little act of violence, perpetrated constantly by the suit- and sweatpants-wearing men of the world, when I watched the beginning of Sergio Leone's *A Fistful of Dynamite* (1971). Like *The Wild Bunch*, the film opens with ants—in this case, a close-up shot of some ants crawling through the nooks and crannies of a chunk of desert rock. They don't look friendly; they look like the red devils that can ruin a camping trip. But then, all of a sudden, they become victims, washed away in a Biblical flood that gurgles and foams and makes them lose their purchase on the rock and tumble down. The camera cuts back and shows us the source of the mayhem: It's a man, a barefooted peasant—a revolutionary, we find out later, fighting to overthrow the corrupt government—taking a piss. You could argue that his piss symbolizes an act of cleansing violence: all the little red tormenters taken out by one purifying deed. But it might also symbolize the opposite. The ants could be the revolutionaries themselves—the diligent collective unable to avoid being pissed on by larger giants that bestride the land.

Like *A Fistful of Dynamite* and many other Westerns (*The Wild Bunch* included), *Red Dead*'s middle chapter takes place in an imagined version of the Mexican Revolution, a real-life conflict that raged from roughly 1910 to 1920. Like many American gunslingers before him, Marston finds himself stepping into the conflict both unwittingly and self-interestedly, with no particular moral stake, siding with whoever promises to give him information as to the whereabouts of Javier Escuella. He starts by doing missions for Captain Vincente de Santa, a vicious sociopath who, the game not-so-subtly implies, derives his sadistic streak from repressed desire for other men. De Santa works for the corrupt Colonel Augustin Allende, a caricature of a banana-republic dictator whose chief goals seem to be to squash the Revolución by any means necessary, and to keep his personal harem of peasant girls well-stocked. In one particularly dark mission, "The Demon Drink," Marston unwittingly helps him with the latter by torching an entire village for Allende, allowing de Santa to collect the refugee women left behind.

Marston also works for the revolutionaries, sometimes even at the same time. After he meets Landon Ricketts, the old-timer cowboy, Ricketts implores Marston to help Luisa, a rebel who might be the only pure and courageous soul in the entire country. At her behest he rescues Luisa's fiancé, the revolutionary leader Abraham Reyes, and begins fighting for the cause; he eventually sides with them for good after she sacrifices herself for Reyes, and after de Santa and Allende betray him. With his help, the rebels prevail. They storm the palace in Escalera, massacring battalions of army soldiers. Marston and Reyes catch Allende fleeing in a stagecoach, pull him out and throw him on the ground. You can choose whether to pull the trigger yourself, or let Reyes do it. Either way, he takes credit for an insurrection that largely depended on Marston, and makes it clear that he'll be exactly like the Colonel he sought to depose: selfish, autocratic, misogynistic, corrupt. Reyes and Allende are mirror images of each other: Reyes grew up rich and became a revolutionary; Allende grew up poor and became a despot. In addition to being killers and narcissistic sociopaths, both are rapists and womanizers who view women as the natural spoils of their conquests. In a running gag that runs one too many times, Reyes keeps forgetting Luisa's name, despite the fact that she saves him and adores him. After he ascends to power, Marston reminds him of her sacrifice, and he vaguely remembers a "magnificent girl" who was "like riding a pampas bull."

Red Dead's middle chapter contains some of its most witheringly cynical moments—moments that step beyond even the cynical worldview of GTA games. It's a part of the game that seems almost designed to dissatisfy the player. A Giant Bomb forum thread from 2010 shows some of the frustration it generated among players who were otherwise huge fans of the game in general:

> kelbear: Even though the player has no control over John Marston, the entire second act of the game just left a bad taste in my mouth. I understand that they were trying to paint a picture of the west as a dark and brutal place, but I'm looking for escapism in this /game/. I don't appreciate them taking away control of my character. With so much power at John's fingertips, I would most certainly use it at every opportunity, however I see fit.

> one_2nd: I felt the same. They made it sound as if you could chose [sic] your morality (like in Fable) but really it was chosen for you. That was really the only disappointment I've had about this game.

WalkerTR77: I definitely hated a lot of the choices that were made for you in Mexico. Especially the mission that had you helping to steal a bunch of women from that town, at least let us choose sides. Although I appreciate that there were no clearly defined good guys, just lots of grey areas. Landon Ricketts however, was the complete business.

MiniPato: I should have been able to decide if I wanted to torch the village or not. I already helped kill all the rebels, denying me information on Bill and Javier just because I don't want to torch empty houses is bullshit.

The good people of the Giant Bomb forums have a point: Given Rockstar's capabilities as a developer, it's hard to imagine a good technological or narrative reason that they couldn't have made the Mexico sequence—which is a standalone interlude—a forking path, giving the player an ability to pick sides and determine the outcome.

But in this arena, too, the game taps into a legacy that is deeper and more complicated than it seems. For decades the Mexico Western was the most political form of Western, used by both the right and the left to think about popular insurrections around the world.

Red Dead draws on many tropes from this subgenre: the reluctant American interloper who arrives for personal reasons, plays both sides, and ends up fighting for the cause; the boorish, drunken revolutionary high on his own ego; the association of Hispanic power—on both sides—with unhinged and voracious sexuality. But the game resonates all the more acutely with the Mexico Western's final curdling: the years between the late 60s and early 70s when a subgenre that had been animated by the prospect of working-class revolution became only capable of imagining revolution's pointlessness. *A Fistful of Dynamite* marks that decadent descent into nihilism and depravity. No film feels more like *Red Dead*'s Mexico chapter in its style, sensibility, and soul.

The Mexico Western is almost as old as the Western in general: It goes back to the time of the revolution itself, when a young Hollywood saw opportunity in the political travails of our neighbor to the south, and when, in a strange kind of symbiosis, the revolutionary Pancho Villa sought out Hollywood to create rousing films based on his real-life exploits. The Mexico Westerns that came out of this relationship—such as *The Patriot* (1916), *Viva Villa!* (1934), *Juarez* (1939), and the John Steinbeck-penned *Viva Zapata!* (1954)—lent the revolution a mythic quality, making it as grand as any of the Western themes that graced the screen.

But they also tended to make the *revolutionary* look like a fool. The real-life Villa was both a charismatic politician and an effective military tactician. In film after film, Hollywood depicted Villa instead (or his counterpart, Emiliano Zapata, with whom Villa was sometimes conflated) as an uncouth bandito who's doing it all out of narcissism, greed, or lust. In "Zapata Spaghetti," an analysis of the Mexico Western, Christopher Frayling quotes an exchange from 1934's *Viva Villa!*, one of Hollywood's more notable fictional retellings of Villa's story. In one of the last scenes of the film, the revolutionary asks a New York journalist to supply him with his last words:

> Villa: Hurry, what were my last words?
>
> Jonny Sykes [the journalist]: "Goodbye, my Mexico. Forgive me for my crimes. Remember if I sinned against you it was because I loved you too much."
>
> Villa (as he dies): "Forgive me," Jonny? What I done wrong?

Frayling points out that the key to this scene is not Villa's idiocy, but the fact that the American journalist—a fictional version of the real-life John Reed, to whom

Villa did tell his story—ends up being the true source of Villa's heroism. American intervention, not homegrown activism, is what creates the galvanizing, mythic figure who leads Mexico to political renewal.

As Richard Slotkin notes in *Gunfighter Nation*, this kind of message was the point of most Mexico Westerns before the 60s. They're about how the revolution succeeds when an American outsider (the cowboy), representing American values, inserts himself into the fray. And they convey this message because they reflect broader anxieties about America's ability to throw its weight around ideologically in troubled Third World countries. Especially in a Cold War-era film like *Viva Zapata!* (1954), "Mexico" isn't really Mexico; it's a stand-in for every Third World nation that was fighting for political autonomy in the age of proxy wars and decolonization. Also in 1954, the leftist political theorist Irving Howe set the scene: "The central fact is that we continue to live in a revolutionary age. […] The workers of Europe are consciously anti-capitalist, the populations of Asia and South America anti-imperialist. These are the dominant energies of our time and whoever gains control of them, whether in legitimate or distorted forms, will triumph." Mexico Westerns responded to this situation of geopolitical unrest by portraying the United States as the revolution's crucial silent partner—a force that steps in to lend a sense of true heroism and decency to a political struggle that might otherwise devolve into unchanneled *bandito* wildness.

Villa the narcissist, Villa the fool, reappears in *And Starring Pancho Villa as Himself*, a lavish HBO movie from 2003 that reflects more extensively (and in a more meta way) on Villa's desire to transform himself into Hollywood myth. Antonio Banderas plays a version of Villa full of preening swagger and a strange kind of naïveté—the hubris of someone already trying on the gilded robes of myth, already saving a parking spot on Olympus, boasting like Beowulf before he even does anything. He strikes a deal with Hollywood to film one of his battles, thinking that it'll make him an immortal star. The battle does not go as he intended; what was supposed to be a decisive skirmish becomes a prolonged siege. But the camera is there to watch him as he smiles for it between gunshots—as he carries around an idea of the present moment, and of what the past will look like to an appreciative future, without much care for the present itself. The camera is there to watch him as he executes the widow of one of his enemies, point-blank, in cold blood.

This version of Villa, Hollywood's Villa, was almost certainly one of the inspirations for Abraham Reyes. Like Villa, Reyes is a terribly human character who basks in the light of his own potential mythology. He boasts constantly of the *corridos*—heroic ballads—that will be written of his exploits, eliding the fact that

Marston tends to be the one who killed hundreds of Federales with a pistol from behind a dingy barrel. As in the Mexico Westerns of old, it is ultimately incumbent upon Marston, the American, to keep Reyes on track, to help him up when he's drunk, and to make sure that his revolutionary force prevails.

Even if it regurgitates the old Villa character, however, *Red Dead* is more interested in a new kind of Mexico Western that emerged in the 1960s, when the Western as a whole became not only darker but also more leftist in its political orientation. In an interview with Frayling, Jean-Luc Godard's collaborator J.P. Gorin remarked that "every Marxist on the block wanted to make a Western" in the 60s. European directors in particular became interested in using the plight of Native Americans, or mine workers, or Mexican peasants, as an allegory for the struggle for civil rights or the tribulations of a suppressed proletariat. With this leftward turn came a new crop of movies about the Revolution that flipped the old template on its head, emphasizing the heroism of the revolutionary as well as the pointless destructiveness of the Americans who insert themselves into another country's business.

A Fistful of Dynamite came out of this trend. The film announces its politics with an epigraph from Mao Zedong himself, pasted starkly in all-caps on a black screen:

THE REVOLUTION

IS NOT A SOCIAL DINNER

A LITERARY EVENT,

A DRAWING

OR AN EMBROIDERY;

IT CANNOT BE DONE WITH

ELEGANCE

AND COURTESY

THE REVOLUTION

IS AN ACT OF VIOLENCE…

The movie does not fail to live up to the promise of its epigraph. Just as *Red Dead* begins with a train full of haughty corseted elites condemning the "savagery" of frontier life, *Dynamite* opens with a stagecoach full of aristocrats shit-talking the peasantry. After a bedraggled hitchhiker—the man who was taking a piss in the opening scene—boards the coach, the film inhabits his POV as the aristocrats disparage the proletariat as "animals" and "brutes," and talk about how the revolution needs to be put down. The film keeps cutting dizzily between their smug, food-stuffed mouths while their insults echo, over and over, in his head. But then there's a twist: He is one of those peasants, and he's here for revenge. He kills most of them; the others, he ties up and humiliates. This brutal, over-the-top spectacle of class insurrection ends with a moment of vile depravity: He exposes his penis to one of the aristocratic women and says, "That's pretty good, huh?"

Focusing on this character, Juan, as well as his white but conspicuously un-American counterpart, a former Irish Republican Army fighter named John, the film gorges the viewer with scenes of insurrectionist violence. Juan and John blow up a military garrison, blow up a bridge while the army is crossing it, fight their way into the center of the capital (a place very reminiscent of *Red Dead*'s Escalera) where propagandistic images of the Governor, hands outstretched toward the people, are pasted on every building. As the city descends into chaos, they end up running into the Governor on the same train, almost by accident. Juan kills him and emerges as a hero, stepping into a literal mosh pit. And yet, in the midst of all the adulation, his blood chills and his face contorts into a terrified expression: What comes next? Have we really achieved anything? Will anything be able to rise from the ruins we have made?

At no point does the movie express doubt that Juan and John are on the right side, or doing the right thing. And yet *Dynamite* overshadows every moment of cathartic violence with the dark possibility that all these revolutionary energies are being corrupted, mischanneled, and ultimately wasted. Although John, the more militant of the two protagonists, ultimately radicalizes Juan a little bit and convinces him to care about what he's doing, Juan still spends most of the film believing that revolutions are "bullshit," and articulating this idea to the audience:

> I know all about the revolutions and how they start. The people that read the books go to the people that don't read the books and say it's time to have a change. And they sit around the polished table and they talk and talk and eat and eat and what has happened to the poor people? They're dead.

Later events do little to contradict his view: Hundreds of people die, the bank vault they rob ends up being empty, and the revolutionary leader they were fighting for—a nerdy, bespectacled doctor—ends up being a traitor to the cause. The movie ultimately vindicates Juan, and its tone oscillates between rage and nihilism, glee and cynicism, giddy excitement and an almost catatonic kind of despair.

That's the tone of *Red Dead*'s Mexico chapter. At no point does the game want you to question Luisa's convictions, or question Marston's decision to fight with her against a man, Allende, who rapes and kills and burns entire villages to the ground, who "runs this place like a feudal king," in the words of Ricketts. But the game overshadows her righteousness with a prevailing sense of futility, written into the landscape—those huge, impossible mesas that bear down upon the ant-like humans—as well as the body language of Marston himself. He's the outsider, the third party, blocking our ability to plug into the game's feeble scenes of political action. He'll never be more than a hired hand, and he'll never let you start thinking that any of this shit will work. After one mission, Reyes gives a speech about returning the land to the people, and creating "a noble republic, justly ruled by noble men." "We will fight on day and night until local tyrants like Allende are no more," Reyes says. "This time things shall be different for every man and woman in this land." As the rebels cheer, Marston just stands there, silently, turns his back and walks away. The effect is sort of like dramatic irony: when you know something that characters in a story don't. But what you know is bleak, overwhelming. It's not just that the game doesn't let you pick sides. It doesn't want you to believe in anything.

Dynamite promises that the very foundations of the world can be changed, blown up, eventually remade. In Leone's film, it becomes almost a kind of fetish object for revolutionary aspirations, containing the hopes and dreams of the disenfranchised proletariat. In a trailer, Juan keeps a little Virgin Mary-like shrine with a picture of the state bank he wants to rob. John pours nitroglycerine into a vial and puts it in the *ofrenda*, like holy water. In *Red Dead*, the revolutionaries also look to dynamite for a way of taking a bite out of the literal and figurative structure of things. In "Father Abraham," one of the missions for Luisa, she tells Marston that her father has been killed by the government: "The army found him and accused him of treason. They cut out his heart and fed it to their dogs." She asks Marston to ambush an army convoy with dynamite planted in the ground: a small act of violence that nevertheless represents the rebellion of the earth itself against the imperial boots that trod upon it.

But dynamite also raises the question of whether the structure of things—political, social, economic—is, in the final count, immutable. What if it's made of even deeper, harder stuff? Video games like *Red Dead* offer an even more potent metaphor for this problem: You can only blow up what you're supposed to, as ordained by the gods of programming. The rest is unbreachable terrain. Luisa asks Marston to make her father's death "mean something." Marston thinks that making it mean anything is impossible: "It'll mean that war is brutal and unnecessary and good people die and that's all it will mean." His answer might feel cynical and heartless in the moment, but the game, like the film, has a way of proving him right.

HISTORY

Before Clint Eastwood, before John Wayne, before *The Virginian*, before any of the Western's 19th-century granddaddies, there was a novel that embodied one of the genre's core ideas: *Don Quixote*. Cervantes's novel anticipates the Western not just because it's about a horse-riding hero, but because it's about a guy who *thinks* he's a horse-riding hero. Don Quixote is an obscure, fifty-year-old man who lives in the middle of Spain, and whose life is defined by middleness: He's middle-class, middle-aged, and thoroughly mediocre. But he reads a lot of books about noble knights saving noble ladies, and he imagines himself sallying forth into their world—a heightened world of old-fashioned heroism, out of joint with his time. In books of chivalry he finds an ideal, and uses it to escape the real. Of course, the real always finds a way to catch up with him, like when he plunges his lance into a windmill, thinking it's a giant.

You could read the whole history of the Western as a series of variations on the Don Quixote problem—on the gap between the world as it is and the world that an idealist like Don Quixote imagines it to be. Classical Westerns thrive on the difference between the chivalric ideal they depict and the modern, degenerate real world inhabited by the viewer. Like Quixote, we want to enter them, if only to experience something higher—purer— than the compromises of our daily lives. By contrast, revisionist Westerns get their kicks by deflating the ideal, and by confronting us with a "real" West that torpedoes all the stereotypes. They tell us that the cowboy was not so nice, that the frontier was only ever a real place of decay and suffering, that the "Myth of the West" is now dead, or was never alive to begin with. Postmodern Westerns like *Westworld* tell us something all the more unsettling. The West was never real; it was only ever our fantasy. It can only ever be a virtual realm for latter-day Don Quixotes to scamper around in, only to end up finding that their real lives are illusory, too.

Does *Red Dead* take us to the real or the ideal—to the real West or a fantasy world? At many points, characters insist on the reality of their world in contrast to other versions of the West that exist in the imagination. Riding with Marston, MacDougal muses about his old illusions: "You know, I dreamt of documenting the last days of the Old West. The romance, the honor, the nobility! But it turns out it's just people killing each other." To which Marston replies: "It always was,

Professor. And the old West ain't quite dead yet." Later in the game, Marston tells his son to get his nose out of the dream of the West that resides in dime novels:

> Jack: I read this story about a girl who was raised by wolves. And she'd hunt goats with them and everything.
>
> Marston: Sounds like a tall yarn to me.
>
> Jack: Taller than a boy being taken from his home and locked up in a dungeon?
>
> Marston: I'm just sayin', maybe you spend too much time with your head in those books.
>
> Jack: I thought you and Ma wanted me to read?
>
> Marston: We do. So long as you're not, well, hidin' from the real world.
>
> Jack: It's a little late for that, Pa.

MacDougal and Marston's son couldn't be more different, but they are alike in one respect: In both cases, an absorption in books has left them with notions about the West of which they must be disabused. Marston, ever the realist, is the one who gives them the reality check.

But several characters throughout the game give *him* a reality check, and they tend to do it in similar ways: by reminding him not that they live in the real world, nor even that they live in a hard and degrading place, but that they live in *history*, and there is no escape from its flow. "I'm not a politician," says Marston to Captain De Santa, as a way of justifying his flip-flopping between the Revolución and the state. "I'm not a soldier," the captain replies, "but we are both beholden to our time." In a similar scene, Reyes, de Santa's political nemesis, asks Marston a question: "Have you ever had the feeling that you are living history?" "Ain't we all livin' history?" Marston replies.

The third iteration of this idea comes from Luisa, later on—and when she says it, even though she has done much more to affect the course of history than Reyes has, it rings with a certain truth.

"I am living in history," she says. "I am not afraid to die."

•

What would it mean to live in history within a video game? Even ten years ago, this question wouldn't have been particularly worth asking. Many (perhaps even most) video games are ahistorical, not only in their subject matter but in the experience they offer. There is no time in *Super Mario Bros.*—only the time you have to complete the level. There is no time in Zelda, either, despite the Temple of Time and with the exception of the oppressive clock tower in Majora's Mask; the series puts its players in spaces of myth, frequently trafficking in images of suspended animation. If anything, games like these seem to offer an escape from history, aligning with Nietzsche's assertion, in his 1874 essay "On the Use and Abuse of History for Life," that true happiness is achieved by forgetting. In the essay he glares jealously at the way animals live in an eternal present, unburdened by the weight of the past:

> Observe the herd which is grazing beside you. It does not know what yesterday or today is. It springs around, eats, rests, digests, jumps up again, and so from morning to night and from day to day, with its likes and dislikes closely tied to the peg of the moment.

Many games give us something close to what Nietzsche describes—a relief from the experience of time. When you stop playing, you might be surprised that it's dark outside, or light outside, and your life has moved on without you. A friend of mine used to describe long sessions of *Civilization V* as "time travel."

To be sure, history is the explicit subject of Civilization, and other strategy game series like it: Crusader Kings, Age of Empires, etc. But they don't really bring you *into* history. If anything, they let you remain outside it as a puppeteer and a presiding god. These games represent—and allow you to remix—the entire history of the world, but by design they only let you view it panoramically, macroscopically, and macroeconomically. History becomes a matter of strategic resources, geopolitical jostling—barren deserts and fertile crescents. The lives of people appear only in the form of abstract statistics (for example, *Civ V*'s "happiness" metric) or a text bubble informing you that building the Library of Alexandria was a huge success.

In the last decade, however, the rise of the big-budget open world game has brought with it a cohort of historical epics that promise to put you *in* history, rather than dictating it from above. Enough of them have come out for an enterprising gamer to be able to play through almost the entire history of mankind—or at least a very stereotypical version of Western History's Greatest Hits. The Assassin's Creed franchise alone has entries that cover ancient Greece, Ptolemaic Egypt, the Crusades, the Renaissance, the American Revolution, the French Revolution, Victorian England, and the golden age of 18th century piracy. Rockstar's games have mapped most of the 20th century in America through depictions of major urban centers: LA in the 40s, 90s, and 2010s; Miami in the 80s; New York in the 2000s. Every one of these games has attempted to recreate a different setting in loving, studious detail, with years of development spent copying architecture, combing through archives, and consulting with academics.

It's easy to dismiss these games as not being interested in history per se. They might tell a good story against a historical backdrop, or simply use the rooftops and boulevards of old places as exotic playgrounds for the player. But they're also a lot bigger, a lot more ambitious as simulations, than we tend to give them credit for. A few months after *Assassin's Creed Origins* came out, Ubisoft released a new mode called Discovery Tour, a kind of living museum where the player can simply move around the game's lavish simulation of Ptolemaic Egypt and read informative blurbs about objects, places, and people. On one level, the mode reorients the player's attention toward the sheer amount of labor that goes into a game like *Origins*, which regular gameplay can otherwise obscure. With awe, and maybe a little bit of horror, you can gain a deep appreciation for the months and months of work that hundreds of developers across multiple continents spent simply *building* this place. But the mode also reminds us that *Origins* really is a way of writing history, even if it's an Assassin's Creed game.

It's an attempt to immerse us in the sensory world of another time.

Because *Red Dead* is so cinematic, so steeped in the audiovisual language of a genre that presents mythic places, elemental conflicts, and larger-than-life heroes, the game has a quirky relationship to historical realism. It isn't as obsessed with realism as *Red Dead 2*, which presents uncanny facsimiles of archival photos in every loading screen, and strives to feel like a huge, living diorama. It doesn't ask you to drink coffee from a tin cup, or heave the broken wagon wheel onto an immobilized horse-drawn carriage. Instead it has places like Casa Madrugada—a brothel nestled into the shadow of a Mexican canyon that feels like an eternal movie set. Its name means "House of the Rising Sun." Its purpose seems to be to await the arrival of an epic gunfight—a montage set to the song.

Still, *Red Dead* can be hauntingly effective at conjuring a sense of both place and time—or at conjuring a sense of time *because* it has such a strong and suggestive sense of place. A lot of that sense of place comes from objects. The rude, crooked fence along the pathway in front of Manzanita Post. The clothesline that sways in the breeze in the middle of Escalera, embodying a desire for the routine, for continuity, even as people die by firing squad just a few buildings away. Or even some of the stuff that you can see in front of Casa Madrugada:

the destitute look of a cart without a horse, signaling the inevitable abandonment of more savory forms of moneymaking. In *The Ideas in Things*, Elaine Freedgood talks about how it's the unremarkable objects in novels that bring us to another world, because they attest silently to the larger forces that have determined the shape of daily life. "The knowledge that is stockpiled in these things," Freedgood writes, "bears on the grisly specifics of conflicts and conquests that a culture can neither regularly acknowledge nor permanently destroy." Objects are windows into the subconscious of a place. In *Red Dead*, they're windows into past sins, but also a strange yet potent mixture of residual hope and increasing hopelessness—Puritan idealism and corrosive cynicism—that bubbles beneath the surface of the game's present.

When historical open world games work, they show us history in this way, through objects and spaces charged with meaning. They strive for texture and immersion; they break gameplay into accidental anecdotes in which you wander the streets, visit shops, and interact with a sprawling population of ordinary digital citizens. The nature of the period becomes manifest in the sound of a butcher hocking his wares, in the shadows cast by gas lamps, in the dust of an unpaved road. They tell history through stuff—as did Walter Benjamin, whose *Arcades Project* was a gigantic, unfinished attempt to contain the spirit of 19th century Paris in an archaeology of unremark-able text fragments. Or Thomas Carlyle, who believed he could excavate a sense of the French Revolution by looking closely at its detritus.

Or even Herodotus, often recognized as the first historian in the Western tradition, who believed that he could give his reader a better sense of why the Persian Wars happened by looking at the details and customs of different places. Whereas his successor, Thucydides, would go on to tell the story of the Peloponnesian War as one unified saga with a single narrative thread and identifiable heroes and villains (generals, statesmen, traitors), Herodotus was the master of the seemingly random digression. He might spend several pages recounting the origin story of a single pot, or retelling a folktale about a man who rode a dolphin from Sicily to Corinth, or explaining why Egyptian women pee stand-ing up. But his point was that the "customs" of places can drive the course of history much more than individ-ual actions, because cultural context informs individual actions in powerful and often invisible ways. *Assassin's Creed Origins* is peppered with Herodotus quotes. In *Assassin's Creed Odyssey* he appears as an actual character you can interact with, and provides the pretext for the story: The player's modern-day avatar, researcher Layla Hassan, has discovered a long-lost Herodotean volume that documents the exploits of the player's ancient avatar, a former Spartan soldier. It makes sense that Herodotus would be the patron saint of these games, because what they try to achieve through the open-world form is a lot like what he tries to achieve in text. He's the master of parataxis, which in Greek means "the art of putting things side by side": the major next to the minor; the deeds of kings next to small and strange and seemingly inconsequential details. In a similar way, open world games urge their players to pursue minor things and place the major on hold, theoretically giving them a more detailed and bottom-up picture of the forces and tensions—economic, geographic, sociopolitical, religious—that define a period.

Yet *Red Dead* might capture this Herodotean quality even better than Assassin's Creed, because it avoids a contradiction at the core of AC games: the way they let you pretend to live in history, but also give you power over it—sometimes godlike power. Even though they offer a materialist history of the mundane, even though they let you run around and take in the texture of another time and draw different conclusions about what happened and *why* it happened, AC games almost inevitably end up offering a history of Great Men and Great Deeds, or what Nietzsche calls a "monumental" history of powerful individuals and willful action. They almost inevitably end up having linear plots that emphasize the world-historical agency of individual figures—chief among them, the player. It helps that the protagonist in AC games also tends to be someone with "Isu" DNA, genetically related to an ancient race of superhumanoids with superior climbing and combat skills.

True, AC games never seem to put you in the position of a king or a president or a general; they tend to have protagonists that are more like Zelig or Forrest Gump, appearing almost accidentally at crucial turning points, determining what happens in indirect, invisible ways. But you're still unmistakably an agent of historical change, even if you generate it by subtly influencing (or eliminating) the more canonical figures you run into. One of the first historical novels in English, Walter Scott's *Waverley* (1814), is about a disaffected, bumbling young aristocrat who—by virtue of being in the right place at the right time, or the wrong place at the wrong time—ends up affecting the course of the Jacobite rebellion. AC games follow a similar mold. But they're also allergic to the idea of incompetence. There is perhaps no better Gamer Power Fantasy than the enfranchisement of the invisible badass, turning the wheels of history and being recognized not by historians, but by other Great Men.

The incoherence of AC games stems from the very problem that makes them fun to play in the first place. We *want* to be able to change history, and we're afraid that we can't. We seek out these games because we want to do something more than just live, day-to-day, in this time or any other time. If AC games eventually succumb to the kind of linear Great Man narrative they seem to resist, it may be because the enfranchisement of the invisible badass is too tempting a proposition. Even Herodotus, for all his digressions, found himself succumbing to the current of print: its tireless linear flow, which turns anything into a story of kings and deeds eventually.

Red Dead succumbs, too. It has a beginning, middle, and end. It has a protagonist who *feels* enfranchised, with his own godlike power to kill with impossible efficiency. It isn't just a diorama that you can run around in; it's a personal narrative that unfolds against the backdrop of much larger political, social, and economic developments. But the pains it takes to register the vastness of those developments—their churning inexorability—might be what makes it work as a representation of historical experience. There is no stepping out of history through superhuman DNA, a sci-fi plot device that turns the past into a simulation (AC's Animus), or any other shortcut. There is no pivotal, epoch-making figure to save, influence, or kill. There is no fantasy of escape to latch onto like a security blanket, as the world around you transforms. There is only living in history—and not being afraid to die.

•

"The Western," says film critic Jim Kitses, "incarnates history." In a literal sense it's easy to understand what he means. Most Westerns are period pieces that want to bring us into another time. They want to immerse us in a time that was modern but not too modern—freer than our own time, but not for long. They want us to smell the leather and hear the horses and feel the splintery wood. What Kitses also means, though, is that Westerns make historical arguments, and encase a theory of American history in their bones. They tell a story about how we got here and where we're headed next—as well as what we had to overcome.

That story is usually a variation on Turner's Frontier Thesis, retold in an elegiac key. America grew up by heading West, into the wild, continually meeting challenges and reinventing itself on the threshold between savagery and civilization. Its character was forged in the crucible of constant struggles: against beasts, against the elements, against (implicitly) racial Others. But then the frontier closed, and so, too, did our opportunities for self-making. We stalled out, lost our way. Any progress we make now is a way of wandering from our path and forgetting who we are.

Why do Westerns incarnate this idea? Why do they try so hard to make us feel it? Fears burn in the engine of the genre—fears of modernity, of urbanism, of immigrants, of women. But Westerns also embody another fear, which comes with another theory of history: the fear that we, as Americans, are doomed to never again be the protagonists of our own story.

The cowboy is a paradox. On the one hand, according to the Frontier Theses of both Turner and Roosevelt, he represents one of American history's purest and most consequential protagonists, carrying forward the struggle of the pilgrims into new and ever more hostile lands of promise. On the other hand, he's always a dinosaur, a dying breed. He will be swept into the dustbin of history; he has no ability to stem the tide. The cowboy might do something noble, like saving the lives of a mother and child (as Eastwood does in *A Fistful of Dollars*), but his time is running out, and his best option is ultimately to run away. He's not the kind of hero who will be able to fight the barbarians at the gate. The irony and the tragedy is that his agency in one era creates his impotence in another. By cleansing the town of outlaws, by winning his various contests against the forces of the wilderness, he only makes it that much easier for the federal government—or the railroad company, or some other large, predatory, colonizing force—to move in. Through his actions, he helps drive the engine of American progress forward, only ensuring that he will become the flattened victim of its Westward march.

Even a movie as seemingly removed from history as *The Good, The Bad, and the Ugly*—with its allegorical trio of characters and its almost mythic texture—dwells on this paradox. The film's three central figures have no particular stake in the Civil War that is erupting around them; their conflict is about a cache of gold, pure and simple. Their cat-and-mouse game takes them to a town under siege, an already-fragile frontier settlement being pulverized by cannon fire, and as the battle rages on, they burrow and weave through the ratholes like Snake at the beginning of *Metal Gear Solid 4*, using the war for cover. At the end of this sequence, Eastwood looks at the battle and says, "I've never seen so many men wasted so badly"—a truism spoken from a position of detachment. Because he's on no side, he can comment on the folly of both sides. Because he's the Good, beholden to a higher code, he can remain outside politics and outside history. And yet the mere presence of the Civil War as a backdrop only raises the question: Is such a detachment even possible? He, too, will get caught up in the sweep of things. In the film he seems irrelevant and a little bit pathetic, chewing on his cigar and playing in the cemetery while the people around him die.

The cowboy's relationship to history inverts his relationship to the world—his command of the plains, his ability to straddle them atop his high and mighty horse.

He can control space, but he can never control time. His drama plays out in an era when, as Kitses puts it, "options are open," and the frontier is not yet closed. But his final tragedy is generated by the imminence of their closure, and the inexorable dawning of an era when options are few and far between. Like a Rorschach blot, he can represent different forms of historical impotence for different groups of people. If you're on the left, he might represent the final foreclosure of the ability to resist, to create change, to band together into a meaningful coalition against the hegemonic march of Progress. If you're on the right, he might represent the erosion of an old value system, the death of chivalry, or the last free man unbound to the albatross of an overbearing centralized government. If you're a woman or a native or a person of color, the death of the cowboy might be good riddance: Too often the cowboy, however much he lacks agency, is still actively complicit in systems of oppression that prevent marginalized people from having any agency to begin with. Too often, nostalgia *for* the cowboy is really nostalgia for colonialism—for a world that openly gave agency to some at the direct expense of others. Even so, the problem of historical agency plays out on the screen before the Western's viewers, inviting them to contemplate the forms of disempowerment that they experience, day to day, in the world just beyond the Western's historical horizon. The whole point of the frontier is that its much-vaunted freedoms are illusory, contingent, and time-sensitive—open to some people now, open to no one in good time.

Then again, just because the cowboy lacks agency over history doesn't mean that he remains outside it. He represents something else at the same time: the way we cannot help but be historical agents anyway. We contribute—in ways that are often subtle, sometimes invisible—to the very changes and systems of oppression that leave some of us feeling alienated and disempowered and leave others feeling all the more so. In the essay "Stranger in the Village," a meditation on the tenacity and inevitability of racism, James Baldwin writes that "people are trapped in history, and history is trapped in them." It is as foolish to believe that we can dictate history as it is to believe that we're not part of it.

Red Dead represents Baldwin's idea in a uniquely powerful way: through the agency of the player. Player agency and historical agency are negative images of each other: You can do plenty as Marston, but Marston can't do anything in the larger scheme of things. The two halves of this equation complement each other; the player's capabilities only heighten the pathos of Marston's historical incapability. And in another ironic twist, Marston really does become an agent of the progress that is his annihilation—performing the government's clean-up operations, stamping out the last vestiges of resistance, and doing his part to close the frontier once and for all.

In *Hamlet on the Holodeck*, her prophetic 1997 study of digital narrative, Janet H. Murray observed that one thing games are good at doing, or at least capable of doing, is giving the player a sense of agency. The linear medium of print, the participatory medium of theater: All have tried, in one form or another, to give the reader or spectator an ability to change things, but digital worlds take that promise to a whole new level, as players tend to intuitively recognize. Video games are so interactive, so immersive, and so player-centric that they almost inevitably inculcate the expectation that we will have power within them. "[T]he more realized the immersive environment," Murray writes, "the more active we want to be in it." But agency is not the same as interactivity. Just being able to move an avatar around and do things with the controller is not the same as having a meaningful effect on the world, and the same desire that games with immersive worlds produce is often the one that they most frustrate. "The desire for agency in digital environments makes us impatient when our options are so limited," she writes. That players of *Red Dead* would be frustrated by the Nuevo Paraíso sequence illustrates her point. *Red Dead* doesn't just fit into a game genre that, more than any other genre, promises freedom. It also taps into the deep appeal of a movie genre that idealizes freedom above all else: freedom to roam, to kill, to be unbridled by norms and rules.

Being free to do things is not the same as being able to change things. This is what *Red Dead* ultimately conveys, and what it conveys most acutely through Marston's death scene. After nine missions at the ranch—nine missions in which you get to pretend, as Marston, to experience the dull pleasure of an untroubled and unadventurous life—the government comes knocking. They never stopped hunting you. They only wanted you to let your guard down. They show up as silhouettes on the horizon: men, countless men, the full force of the law. For a time, the game makes you think you can withstand them. They come from all sides, but you can use any tool at your disposal to dispatch them one by one. You also get to choose whether to stay on the ground, fighting them head-on, or climb up to the corn silo to snipe them. No matter what you do, though, you'll end up with Jack and Abigail in the barn, at which point there begins a scene made for melodrama. Marston puts them on a horse, tells them to "keep ridin' and don't look back." "You stay out of trouble, John," she says; "Ain't no trouble," he replies. In a moment that feels like the climax to a million other movies, he kisses her for the last time and slaps the horse: "Now go! Git!"

He swaggers toward the double doors of the barn, opens a crack and sees the men with guns ready for him, biding their time. The camera looks at him head-on, capturing one eye through the crack, and for a second it looks like one of Eastwood's eyes in so many of those close-ups: grim, stoic, determined. But then it softens, ever so subtly, into an expression of fear and recognition. It's the end of the line. He takes a step back, takes a deep breath, and shoves open the double doors. In one of the game's most ingenious moments, Dead Eye bathes the soldiers in yellow and gives you a chance to kill them all—maybe if you're fast enough, maybe if you're good enough. Of course, there's no way to win, and within seconds, the action cuts to Marston's body, riddled with bullets, collapsing to the ground. It takes a long time for his knees to buckle, for the last coughs to escape his throat, for the gun to fall out of his hand. The death feels gratuitous, almost ritualistic—completely unlike the random (and much more believable) bodily traumas that Euphoria inflicted upon him throughout the rest of the game. But that may be the point. Euphoria no longer has jurisdiction. *You* no longer have jurisdiction. Dead Eye and Euphoria both represent forms of freedom finally crushed under the weight of an inexorable determinism, a prewritten script. Larger forces authored that script, but Marston is also, in many ways, its co-author: Everything you do as him brings him closer to this moment. And everything you do as Jack, his successor, is a reiteration of the same old story.

If player choice is one of the "affordances" (to borrow Murray's term) of the digital medium that video games can use to create meaning, *Red Dead* shows us that lack of choice—lack of *agency*—can be just as meaningful, especially at the end of an open experience. There's something powerful about reaching the end of a massive labyrinth and finding yourself faced with a wall, or a mirror, or the beginning of the labyrinth all over again. *Westworld* explores a similar idea, juxtaposing the open world of the park against the determinisms of android programming and human nature. Many other Westerns explore the same idea when they depict the cowboy getting swept inexorably into the history he's trying to avoid.

So what kind of history is *Red Dead Redemption*? In his 1974 book *Metahistory*, the theorist and historian Hayden White argues that every work of history, on some level, fits into the familiar cultural molds that we use to tell stories: comedy, tragedy, epic, farce. Many historical narratives make meaning out of their source material by shaping it into "romance," a kind of quest narrative that presents not only "the triumph of good over evil," but also the hero's personal transcendence over the injustices that consume the world. *Red Dead* would seem to opt for tragedy instead—a version of history premised on the inevitable downfall of its participants. Yet the game feels more like something else he describes as "satire":

> The archetypal theme of Satire is the precise opposite of this Romantic drama of redemption; it is, in fact, a drama of diremption, a drama dominated by the apprehension that man is ultimately a captive of the world rather than its master, and by the recognition that, in the final analysis, human consciousness and will are always inadequate to the task of overcoming definitively the dark force of death, which is man's unremitting enemy.

"Diremption" means a severing, a cutting in two—a destruction of the hero by the world that is his captor, the world he will never be able to overcome. This idea is all over the place in *Red Dead*. It's at the core of the game's narrative of inescapable self-erasure. It's at the core of Marston's ceaseless killing and dying under the unforgiving sun. It's there at the beginning of Marston's story, when he emerges in handcuffs to embark on his doomed and pointless quest; it's there especially at the end, when he looks through the door and sees the executioners, and his determination melts into sadness. If *Red Dead* is "satire," it's a deeper and more bitter kind than the cynical jabs Rockstar has always been known for. But it might be the best kind: the kind that reminds us of the absurdity of our place within history, and the folly of our attempts to command it, get out in front of it, or look at it from the outside.

"God, grant me the serenity to accept the things I cannot change, courage to change the things I can, and wisdom to know the difference." So goes Reinhold Niebuhr's "Serenity Prayer," a mainstay of recovery programs in which people seek redemption of another kind. Characters throughout *Red Dead* speak versions of this prayer—not literally, but in their resignation toward history's oppressive weight, its unharnessable vastness. There's Luisa: "I am living in history. I am not afraid to die." And then there's Dutch van der Linde, Marston's egomaniacal nemesis: "We can't always fight nature," he says. "We can't fight change. We can't fight gravity. We can't fight nothing. My whole life, all I ever did was fight." He says this after Marston finally catches up with him—after *history* finally catches up with him, in the form of a man it will also destroy. Dutch says this right before he decides to jump.

"People are trapped in history, and history is trapped in them." Luisa embraces it; Dutch accepts it; *Red Dead* shows it. Yet the game's most provocative effect might be the way it hides that truth, or makes us experience its elusiveness in a world where freedom is so palpable, and agency seems so attainable. The way it uses the illusory freedoms of its design to bring us face to face with illusory freedoms of a larger kind. The way it preaches historical humility through an experience of simulated power. Marston can do so much in this game: rob stagecoaches, hunt buffalo, shoot outlaws, ride across the landscape. You can make him do so many things that shield you from his impotence—from the fact that vast forces have conspired to encase him in his destiny. But the game will always remind you that his lasso is his noose. He can never escape being consumed by the march of progress. You will never escape the gravity of time.

CODA

VIDEO GAMES PLUG THEMSELVES into our lives. They offer escape, but they also offer a strangely appealing kind of companionship. They can be there for us, day after day, ready to soak up our moods and give us something else in return. The nature of that "something" varies. Like long novels, some games give us a world. Like TV shows, some games give us characters. Some games give us no more and no less than "gamefeel": the precise aerodynamics of a jump, or the pleasing friction of a heavy sword swing that lands at just the right moment, or the little *thnk* sound when you nail a headshot. Some games give us sheer grandiosity of scale. That's what I loved about JRPGs in high school—the way their endless grinds and long, nonsensical stories would fill the awkward cracks in my daily life.

When I played *Red Dead* for the first time, it gave me a combination of all those things—the world, the characters, the gunplay, and the massive, almost hubristic scope. I was probably drawn to it for the gamefeel first;

then I got hooked on the sense of exploration and territorial acquisition that comes with the open world; then I stayed for the steady drip of action sequences and well-crafted motion-capture cutscenes that made it feel like a playable movie. But what it gave me most of all were moments that lodged themselves in my brain like slivers of crystal. Leading cattle across the hills and valleys of New Austin while a lightning storm brews overhead. Meeting the Strange Man on the cliff overlooking Armadillo—and meeting him again at Marston's gravesite. Dutch on the cliff, delivering his soliloquy about change. Coming home to Beecher's Hope, meeting Abigail and Jack, and wondering where the game could be going from there. Opening the barn doors, furiously sweeping the soldiers with Dead Eye, and watching Marston die. These were the moments that stuck. And because I was part of them, they lodged ever more forcefully in my brain, becoming part of me.

I played *Red Dead* in college, at an awkward time when I was on the cusp of becoming my own person but still had so many childish ways. When my father still loomed over me, looked after me, but was starting to show his vulnerabilities, and the weakness—alcoholism—that would destroy him. I think some of these moments stuck with me because they struck a chord with my insecurities about masculinity and natal fatalism: the idea that we're doomed to repeat the mistakes of our parents. Yet they also stuck with me because they resonated with something collective, rather than something merely personal. They had the weight of familiar touchstones, even if I'd never been close to the West at all. The familiarity came from intertextuality: the way the game draws so deeply from an old well of images and ideas that has stood there for a long time, and that I'd drank from, many times, without entirely knowing.

When she published *Hamlet on the Holodeck* in 1997, Murray thought about how video games might continue the long legacy of storytelling that has evolved across prior genres, from oral poetry to drama, the novel, radio, movies, and TV. With messianic fervor she awaits the coming of a Hamlet for the digital age—not a translation of *Hamlet* into another format but a "cyberdrama," native to the digital medium yet continuous with the other narrative arts, that "capture[s] something as true to the human condition, and as beautifully expressed, as the life that Shakespeare captured on the Elizabethan stage." There's a fear implicit to her fantasy that seems well-founded in retrospect: All-too-often, games behave as though the older narrative forms don't even exist. Instead, conscious of their own cultural hegemony, they retreat into a kind of terminal self-absorption, as though the worlds they make have become big enough to answer any questions they—or we—might ask. *Red Dead* isn't quite the neo-*Hamlet* Murray was hoping for; sure, it's a tragedy in its own right, but it's not *that* kind of tragedy. Sure, it's good; it's not *that* good. But it shows us the amazing things that are possible when a game tries its best to forge that link to the past, attaching an old genre to the affordances of the digital medium and attaching the digital medium to the heavy weight of an old genre. A genre that is itself, in so many ways, the long, complicated legacy of homegrown American myth.

NOTES

Western

For an incredibly entertaining and well-researched account of *Red Dead Revolver*'s vexed development, see Blake Hester's feature in *Polygon*, "How the Red Dead Franchise Began," October 17, 2018: https://bit.ly/2ZBwlBG.

Rockstar co-founder Dan Houser incited controversy in October 2018 when he praised the *Red Dead 2* team for "working 100-hour weeks" in an interview with *New York Magazine*, "How the West Was Digitized: The making of Rockstar Games' *Red Dead Redemption 2*" (https://bit.ly/2u5FZkp).

David Kushner's *Jacked: The Outlaw Story of Grand Theft Auto* (Turner, 2012) remains the best history of early Rockstar, focusing on the years between Sam Houser's childhood and the release of *GTA4*.

For an example of *Red Dead* being labeled "Grand Theft Horse" in the enthusiast press, see: Russ Frishtick, "'Red Dead Redemption' is Basically 'Grand Theft Horse'…And That's a Good Thing," MTV News, December 15, 2009 (https://on.mtv.com/36e1vBM).

The quote from critic Simon Parkin comes from his May 18, 2010 review of *Red Dead* in Eurogamer: https://bit.ly/2F8v77C.

Aristotle discusses tragedy in the *Poetics* (translated by Leon Golden, Prentice Hall, 1968).

The quotes from Christian Cantamessa come from an April 7, 2010 interview with GameFan Magazine, a now defunct video game publication. It's still available via WebCite: https://bit.ly/2SPQ7Iv

J. Hoberman's essay "How the Western Was Lost" originally appeared in *The Village Voice* (August 27, 1991), where he served as head film critic for many years. It can now be found in *The Western Reader* (Limelight Editions, 2010), which is an excellent repository of critical writing on the genre edited by Jim Kitses and Gregg Rickman that I've used extensively throughout this project.

The first André Bazin quote (about the Western being as old as cinema) comes from his 1953 essay "The Western: Or, the American Film Genre *Par Excellence*." The second Bazin quote (comparing *Stagecoach* to a wheel) comes from his second essay on the Western, "The Evolution of the Western," published in 1955. Both were reprinted in the collection *What is Cinema?* vol. 2 (University of California Press, 2005), but the essays are actually very different: In the first, Bazin admires the Western's tenacity and its ability to resist "contaminations" from other genres. In the second, he praises a new breed of "superwestern" that wasn't pure, that was "ashamed to be just itself, and looks for some additional interest to justify its existence." The Western is always the Western—until, somehow, it's not.

Published in 1993 by Oxford University Press, Jane Tompkins's *West of Everything: The Inner Life of Westerns* has been my Bible throughout this project: No one writes about the genre with more eloquence than Tompkins, and no one seems to understand better what its core elements—dust, horses, cowboys, pain—are really about.

Robert Warshow's 1954 essay "Movie Chronicle: The Westerner" was originally published in *The Partisan Review*, but can now be found reprinted in *The Western Reader*. The essay has a horrible title but a lot of crucial insights, especially regarding the allure of the cowboy as an icon.

In his study of John Wayne, *John Wayne's America: The Politics of Celebrity* (Simon & Schuster, 2000), Gary Wills discusses the nature and pervasiveness of the Duke's appeal, including how he became the ideal American in the imaginations of immigrants: "The way to be an American was to be Wayne—a claim given eerie confirmation by the fact that the 1990s Chairman of the Joint Chiefs of Staff, John Shalikashvili, taught himself English, as an immigrant, by watching Wayne movies."

The line from Philip Yordan, Anthony Mann's screenwriter, is quoted in R. Emmett Sweeney's June 17, 2014 FilmStruck blog post "Oedipus West: *The Man from Laramie*," which explores the Greek tragedy overtones of the 1955 film: https://bit.ly/35cvDfe.

Horizons West, Jim Kitses's book-length study of the genre, has been a critical classic since its original 1969 publication by Indiana University Press. One piece of the book that I really like is a chart of comparisons that distills some of the philosophical oppositions that Kitses sees at the Western's core, e.g. "The Wilderness" vs. "Civilisation," "The Individual" vs. "The Community," "freedom" vs. "restriction," "purity" vs. "corruption," and so on.

Territory

The Joseph Addison line is from *Spectator* no. 412 (Monday, June 21, 1712), but I encountered it in David Baker's essay "The Sublime: Origins and Definitions" (*The Georgia Review* vol. 58, no. 2, 2004), which also discusses the contrast between the European sublime (craggy mountains) and the American sublime (endless, expansive space).

Richard Slotkin's *Gunfighter Nation*, originally published in 1992, is the third and final volume in a trilogy of massive books covering the evolution of the idea of the "frontier" in American history, politics, and culture. Slotkin treats 20th century Westerns as the outgrowth of a deep history of American mythmaking, which he traces through *Regeneration through Violence* (covering 1600-1860) and *Fatal Environment* (covering 1800-1890).

Details about Coot's Chapel have been pulled from the *Red Dead* fan wiki: https://bit.ly/2SHqdGC.

In his *Confessions*, Augustine learns about Antony of Egypt, the great ascetic, through the story of another monk who read his biography and was himself inspired to asceticism. The *Inception*-like nestedness of this narrative of spiritual inspiration only underscores Augustine's shameful feeling of distance from the self-denying ideal—the feeling that he can't follow suit. He laments to God about being the scholar, the city-dweller, the sinner, too attached to the world to rid himself of it, anticipating many of the buried feelings of 19th and 20th century cosmopolitans who would look at the cowboy with a strange kind of jealousy (*Confessions*, Oxford World's Classics, 2008).

For more on the Victorian obsession with desert saints, see James Eli Adams, *Dandies and Desert Saints: Styles of Victorian Masculinity* (Cornell University Press, 1995).

Tennyson's poem "Saint Simeon Stylites" can be found in *Tennyson's Poetry*, edited by Robert W. Hill, Jr. (Norton Critical Editions, 1999).

The quote from Dan Houser about *Red Dead* and the "Death of the West" can be found in a May 19, 2010 interview with NowGamer: https://bit.ly/2ZEtwzC.

In his *Arcades Project*, Walter Benjamin treats wrought-iron as both an unmistakable architectural element and a potent symbol of late-19th century modernity. He writes about how it's a step beyond the Greek way of building with rafters, or the medieval way of building with vaulted ceilings: something modern, something new, that embodies the great promise— maybe even the defiance—of a city built from synthetic, rather than natural, materials.

Frontier

Clayton Purdom's indispensable discussion of map games can be found in his February 20, 2017 AV Club essay on *Horizon Zero Dawn*, "Pt. 1—Fighting robot dinosaurs in the woke-as-hell post-apocalypse of *Horizon: Zero Dawn*": https://bit.ly/35ennLH.

The quote from Cameron Kunzelman comes from his April 20, 2017 review of David O'Reilly's *Everything* in Paste Magazine, "*Everything* Is a Game About the Theatrical Artifice of All Games": https://bit.ly/2MCybwX.

Originally published in *Gourmet*, David Foster Wallace's essay "Consider the Lobster" can now be found in the 2005 essay collection of the same title.

Will Partin makes the insightful connection between the experience of playing open world games and Wallace's depressing account of cruise ships in "The Thousand Eyes of *Watch Dogs 2*," Los Angeles Review of Books, February 19, 2017 (https://bit.ly/2Qb7txK).

Frederick Jackson Turner's address "On the Significance of the Frontier in American History," originally delivered to the American Historical Association in Chicago in 1893, can be found reprinted here: https://bit.ly/36bH4VR.

Hoberman devotes some space to describing the absurdities of *How the West Was Won* in "How the Western Was Lost."

Slotkin discusses Kennedy's DNC address—and his invocation of space as the last frontier—at the beginning of *Gunfighter Nation*.

Jedediah Britton-Purdy discusses the vastness of the "infrastructure state" in "Paleo Politics," a review of James C. Scott's *Against the Grain* published in The New Republic, November 1, 2017 (https://bit.ly/35cw1dG).

Death

See Kirk McKeand's 2017 piece in Eurogamer, "Nine Years Later, One Feature in GTA4 Has Never Been Bettered— Here's Its Story," for a more extensive discussion of Euphoria. McKeand's piece includes an illuminating interview with Harry Denholm, former engineering lead at NaturalMotion, who played a large role in implementing Euphoria into *GTA4* and *Red Dead* (https://bit.ly/2QCvHj8).

The quotes from Ted Carson come from a February 10, 2010 interview with GameSpot: https://bit.ly/2Q915a0.

Cowboy

For the history of Dr. Horace Porter and the "Cocoanut Grove" Post Office, see this post at the Miami History Blog: https://bit.ly/2rI5yqX.

Edward Leedskalnin's book—more of a pamphlet, really—is called, grandiosely, *A Book in Every Home*, and online scans of it are floating around the internet (e.g. here: https://bit.ly/2QC7p8Y). Interestingly, the gift shop at Coral Castle does not let you read it before buying it—they sell it shrink-wrapped with a bundle of his other writings. I suspect this is for a reason.

The *BFI Companion to the Western* (BFI, 1988), an extremely useful compendium of Western films, filmmakers, and tropes edited by Edward Buscombe, discusses the significance and the long history of the "good prostitute" archetype. The *Companion* attributes the Western's long history of sympathetic sex workers to two things: "the fantasies of (male) filmmakers," and "the difficulty of finding other interesting and plausible roles for women in a male-dominated genre."

Darwin Payne's biography of Wister, *Owen Wister: Chronicler of the West, Gentleman of the East*, was published by Southern Methodist University Press in 1985.

For more tales of Victorian men traveling to the colonies to escape the enervating effects of industrial, urbanized London, see John Miller's monograph *Empire and the Animal Body: Violence, Identity, and Ecology in Victorian Adventure Fiction*, published by Anthem Press, 2012.

Jess Joho's essay, "The Failure of Masculinity in *Red Dead Redemption*," is the third in an illuminating series of essays on the game published by Bullet Points Monthly, a game criticism publication co-edited by Reid McCarter and Ed Smith. All four of the Bullet Points essays on *Red Dead* have been influential resources throughout this project, including Smith's "Ain't This A Beautiful Spot?", McCarter's "*Red Dead Redemption* Never Escapes the Past" (which I draw from more extensively in Chapter 5), and "Where To Now?" by both Smith and McCarter, a dialogue in which, in the wake of *GTA5*, they discuss the squandered potential of Rockstar's turn from comedy to tragedy between 2008 and 2012. All four essays can be found here: https://bit.ly/2sC91aK.

"The Strenuous Life" was not only a key concept in the mythos of Teddy Roosevelt, but also the subject and title of a famous speech he gave in Chicago on April 10, 1899. Roosevelt extolled "the life of toil and effort, of labor and strife [...] that highest form of success which comes, not to the man who desires mere easy peace, but to the man who does not shrink from danger, from hardship, or from bitter toil, and who out of these wins the splendid ultimate triumph." *Red Dead 2*, even more than the first *Red Dead*, seems designed to ironize Roosevelt and his personal ideology. The game takes place in 1899, features a bearded, rough-hewn Rooseveltian protagonist, and even includes a misadventure into the Caribbean that darkly mirrors the Cuban campaign of Roosevelt's Rough Riders during the Spanish-American War.

Originally published in *Harper's Monthly* in 1895, Owen Wister's article about English aristocrats, "The Evolution of the Cow-puncher," is also quoted in Slotkin's *Gunfighter Nation*.

For more on the history of nonwhite cowboys, see Katie Nodjimbadem's essay "The Lesser-Known History of African-American Cowboys" published on February 13, 2017 by the Smithsonian: https://bit.ly/35bbVjW.

The Pauline Kael quotes are from "Saddle Sore: *El Dorado, The War Wagon, The Way West*," printed in her landmark 1965 essay collection *Kiss Kiss Bang Bang*.

The first George Lucas quote—"I saw the western die"—comes from "George Lucas: The Wizard of 'Star Wars'," an August 25, 1977 interview with *Rolling Stone*: https://bit.ly/2QA1L7k. The second statement, comparing Han Solo to John Wayne, comes from "George Lucas: To feel the true force of 'Star Wars,' he had to learn to let it go," a more extensive and retrospective interview he did with the *Washington Post* in 2015: https://wapo.st/2QBgZcn.

Violence

In his 1967 review of *The Good, the Bad, and the Ugly*, quoted and translated by Christopher Frayling in "Zapata Spaghetti," the Italian novelist Alberto Moravia described the Western's shift from gunfight to "gundown" as part of a larger move toward nihilism pioneered by Italian filmmakers. "After all this, you find yourself asking this question," he wrote. "Just a fistful of dollars? Or is there more?"

Irving Bernstein recounts Lyndon Johnson's 1966 trip to Cam Ranh Bay—and his injunction to the soldiers to "nail that coonskin to the wall"—in *Guns or Butter: The Presidency of Lyndon Johnson* (Oxford University Press, 1996).

Gamelife by Michael W. Clune, which may be the most interesting video game memoir ever written, was published by Farrar, Strauss and Giroux in 2015.

W.J.T. Mitchell discusses the ideological project of Henry Fairfield Osborn, early-20th century director of the American Museum of Natural History, in *The Last Dinosaur Book: The*

Life and Times of a Cultural Icon (University of Chicago Press, 1998)—a hugely entertaining study that often explores how the dinosaur, as a cultural image, has intersected with Western stories and tropes. (*Red Dead 2*'s fossil-finding side mission is an example of this, as is Michael Crichton's recent, posthumously published dino-Western, *Dragon Teeth*).

John Berger's provocative and hugely influential essay "Why Look at Animals?" appears in the 1980 collection *About Looking*.

The quote from General Phil Sheridan comes from *The BFI Companion to the Western*'s informative entry on the history behind large-scale buffalo hunts in the 1870s, as well as their representation in Western films.

Revolution

The story of the Dutch maintenance man who pioneered the fly-in-urinal approach is recounted in the December 19, 2009 NPR story "There's A Fly In My Urinal" by Robert Krulwich: https://n.pr/2QyMKTq.

Christopher Frayling's essay "Zapata Spaghetti: Reflections on the Italian Western and the Mexican Revolution" appears in *Critical Perspectives on the Western: From* A Fistful of Dollars *to* Django Unchained, edited by Lee Broughton (Rowman & Littlefield, 2016).

The Irving Howe passage, from his 1954 essay "The Problem with U.S. Power," can be found quoted in "What Was the

Third World Revolution?", a 2005 essay by the anthropologist Clifford Geertz (*Dissent*, vol. 2, issue 1, Winter 2005).

The quote from Jean-Luc Godard's collaborator J.P. Gorin comes from an interview with Christopher Frayling in his book *Sergio Leone: Something to Do with Death* (University of Minnesota Press, 2012).

The Giant Bomb thread I've quoted from—the original post dates from June 2010, shortly after the game's release—can still be found here as "I'm no moralist sir": https://bit.ly/2u6F9Uv.

History

Nietzsche's essay "On the Uses and Abuses of History for Life" can be found in the collection *Untimely Meditations*, and also here: https://bit.ly/2MI9cIJ.

Elaine Freedgood's *The Ideas in Things: Fugitive Meaning in the Victorian Novel* is an eye-opening exploration of some of the seemingly insignificant objects in the novel's domestic interiors: curtains, mahogany furniture, etc. (University of Chicago Press, 2010).

Thomas Carlyle, a 19th century historian, philosopher, social critic, and Victorian "Sage," practiced his materialist way of writing history in *The French Revolution: A History* (1837). For more on his method, see John McAllister Ulrich, "Thomas Carlyle, Richard Owen, and the Paleontological Articulation of the Past," *Journal of Victorian Culture* vol. 11, no. 1 (2006).

The edition of Herodotus's *Histories* that I've consulted is translated by Robin Waterfield and was published by Oxford World's Classics in 2008.

James Baldwin's essay "Stranger in the Village," originally published in *Harper's Magazine* in 1953, can now be found in the 1955 collection *Notes of a Native Son*.

Hamlet on the Holodeck, Janet H. Murray's study of how the "affordances" of digital technology could reshape narrative art, was extremely prescient when it came out over twenty years ago, predicting all sorts of developments in interactive storytelling (including MMORPGs, interactive TV like *Black Mirror: Bandersnatch,* and, I would argue, the decentralized yet still sort of centralized narratives of open world games). In 2017, the book was reissued by MIT Press, with thoughtful updates to every chapter reflecting on the forms that videogame stories have taken. For more on the reissue and Murray's legacy, see my essay "'Hamlet on the Holodeck,' Twenty Years Later" published August 30, 2017 at the New Yorker: https://bit.ly/39pULT3.

Hayden White's *Metahistory: The Historical Imagination in 19th-Century Europe* was reissued in a 40th anniversary edition in 2014, published by Johns Hopkins University Press. A recent obituary written by Bruce Robbins for *n+1*, "Emancipation from the Burden of History: On Hayden White, 1928–2018," captures what was special about his way of looking at history: https://bit.ly/357Fz9N.

ACKNOWLEDGEMENTS

I STARTED THINKING CRITICALLY about *Red Dead* sometime around April 2016, when I made a throwaway comment about open world games in the Kill Screen Slack (RIP) and my editor, Clayton Purdom, thought there might be something to it. Clayton encouraged me to turn it into an essay for Kill Screen's print magazine (also RIP), which became, in turn, the germ of this book. For that as well as his wisdom, insightful editing, and unbeatable prose style, I'm forever grateful. I'm also grateful for the amazing community of writers in the ex-KS diaspora, who continue to inspire me every day with game criticism that pushes the boundaries of what I thought was possible.

I'm immensely grateful to the editorial team at Boss Fight Books, who made the editing process a joy from start to finish. Thank you to Gabe Durham for reaching out to me, taking a chance on my pitch, and refining the book with thoughtful, incisive feedback; to Michael P. Williams for the eagle-eyed edits and the phrase "hapax legomena"; and to Alyse Knorr for so trenchantly figuring out exactly what the book needed at exactly the right time. I'm grateful as well for all the work put into it by copyeditor Ryan Plummer, proofreaders Joe M. Owens and Nick Sweeney, layout designers Christopher Moyer and Lori Colbeck, and cover designer Cory Schmitz.

As the stuff about the "real and the ideal" at the beginning of Chapter 8 might indicate to a select group of readers, I'm deeply indebted to my students and colleagues at Ransom Everglades School, whose enthusiasm for the project has kept me chipping away at it through many intense, sleepless months. Special thanks to Dr. Kathryn Bufkin and Dr. Gila Aloni for the best of all possible office triumvirates, and to Noah Zaldivar, a young gentleman of considerable literary talent, for generously providing me with a copy of *Red Dead Redemption 2*.

I'm grateful to my mom, for always believing in me, and to my in-laws, Ileana and Ramon Iglesias, for making Miami feel like home. I'm grateful to Eduardo Iglesias for being a hero, and to Anthony Morris for being a prophet. This book wouldn't exist if my way of thinking about literature, politics, and everything else hadn't been shaped by my dad, Lorenzo Margini. May he rest in peace.

Most of all, I'm indebted to Christina, the love of my life. Thank you for reading every single draft, being the best interlocutor I've ever had, and supporting me with your humor, warmth, and brilliance. Thank you for being you, always. And a special thanks to Raymond and Nicholas Margini, the two kings of Sparta, for being just and benevolent rulers. May they never try to hunt a bear.

ALSO FROM
BOSS FIGHT BOOKS